Fat As My Dad

with
Chain Breaking Tips

TIM 2 TAYLOR

Friend Me, Find Me, Tweet Me, See Me
at
#FatAsMyDad and @Tim2Taylor
www.fatasmydad.com

Fat As My Dad
First Printed Edition - 2011
First Digital Edition - 2012
First Audio Edition - 2012

Published by Fat As My Dad, LLC.
7536 Pottsburg Landing Drive
Jacksonville, Florida 32216
www.fatasmydad.com

Written by Tim 2 Taylor
Designed by Tim 2 Taylor
Edited by Tim 2 Taylor

Library of Congress Control Number -

Taylor, Timothy, 1960 -

Manufactured in the United States
ISBN-978-0-9833382-7-7 (book)
ISBN- 978-0-9833382-8-4 (e-book)
ISBN- 978-0-9833382-9-1 (audio book)

SAN 860–1283

Printed by
Lightning Source Inc.
14 Ingram Blvd.
La Vergne, TN USA 37086
1. Weight-loss, Fitness and Health

Distributed by Fat As My Dad, LLC.
To purchase copies in bulk please contact: (904-739-0514)

To book Tim 2 Taylor for personal appearances, book signings or motivational speaking engagements, please call (904) 238-0889
or contact Tim 2 through the website at www.fatasmydad.com

Look for the Fat As My Dad – 2B4L (To Be For Life) Handbook coming soon.

What you believe
about yourself...
it all comes true.

IMPORTANT NOTICE

Although the information contained in this book has been reviewed by a physician, a nutritionist, and other sports specialists, this book reflects the author's personal experiences and personal opinions about weight loss, fitness, and mental health. The author is neither a licensed professional nor a physician.

This book is a reference volume only, not a medical manual. It is never to be mistaken for, referred to as, or act as a replacement for sound medical advice from a licensed physician. The information herein is intended to be an aid to readers in their efforts to change their lifestyles, lose weight, keep excess weight off, and improve their overall health and well-being.

Before starting any nutritional, weight loss or exercise regimen, we strongly encourage you to consult a physician or licensed professional to make sure that you are healthy enough to proceed. You should always get a doctor's approval to begin any diet or exercise program.

Before putting any of the advice given in this book into practice, you should get a complete physical, stress test, and full blood work-up. Do this BEFORE you start putting anything you read in this book into action to be sure it is appropriate for you.

All exercise has inherent risk. We advise you to know your limits, always warm up before and cool down afterwards, and always exercise safely.

No supplements referenced in this book should be taken without consulting your physician or licensed professional. The author does not endorse any company, product, service, or goods mentioned in this book and has not received compensation or consideration from any persons or company mentioned in this book at the time of its writing and publication.

All references to any company, products, services, or goods mentioned in this book were actually used by the author during his weight-loss, and their effectiveness is strictly a matter of the author's opinion.

All logos and names of products, referenced in this book are trademarks of their respective companies.

CONTENTS

This book is dedicated to all the people
who believe that positive change
is always possible.

I would like to thank all the people who have
believed in me throughout my life.

I especially want to thank the special women
(You know who you are.)
who have played such a significant role
in saving my life. Without their love, understanding,
and kindness, I could have never become
the blessed, healthy man I am today.

Thank You!

FOREWARD

"Basket-ball-belly!"

Laughing out loud as only a boy of ten years old can, I pointed at my dad and called out the name again... "Basket-ball-belly." He said, "You better watch out what you call me, because one day it will you being called fatso, tubby, or basket-ball-belly yourself."

Fast forward thirty three years, on one of my dad's yearly pilgrimages to visit me at my home in sunny Florida, it was my own father laughing and calling me...
Basket-ball-belly!

Yep, it had happened. What every man deep inside fears the most, I had become as fat as my dad. How had this happened? When did it happen? How did I let myself get this way? If you're reading this, undoubtably you're asking yourself the same questions. At 18, when I graduated high school, I weighed a whopping 136 pounds. How in the world did I gain 136 pounds in just 27 years? That's an average weight gain of just 5 pounds a year. Basically I'd gained a whole other person in weight. It's hard to believe... but it's absolutely true.

If you're a man over the age of 35, and this sounds similar to your life and you see yourself in this same situation or headed in that direction, I'm glad you picked up this book! I've got some really good news for you.

If you've put on as much or more weight than I had... If you've become as fat as your dad, or are as unhealthy, as sick, or as tired as your dad... or if, God forbid, your father has passed on from poor health... you still have time to change your life forever!

Fat As My Dad isn't a diet book per se. Will it help you lose weight? Yes! Will it help you change your life? Yes! Will it help you to become a better man? I sure hope so! I'm calling it a "Life-It ®" book instead of a diet book.

This book is the inspiring real world story of my weight loss journey (over four years in the making). I've condensed it down to focus on the essential things that really worked for me. I've written it especially to help men over the age of 29 lose weight and change their lives. Women can gain some profound insights and help their boyfriends, husbands or their own dad to become healthier, happier men from reading it, too.

You don't have to read this book from front to back in one sitting. Scan through the chapters until you see a topic that piques your interest and just read that chapter. It's been designed to be absorbed quickly and easily. I believe if you put just four chain breaker tips into your life every 28 days and take action on them, you'll become fitter, healthier, and happier than you've ever imagined.

Tim 2 Taylor

My Fat 2 Thin Journey

Beep, Beep, Beeeeeeeeeee the heart monitor screamed. "Hold on... It will come back!" The EMT said as he flipped a switch and reached for the paddles. Was this the way my life was going to end? In the back of a speeding ambulance? I feared that the last feeling I was going to experience was a horrifying electrical shock to my body. Slow-motion terror overtook me in that second, enveloping me in a surreal dream-like state.

The accumulation of everything I had worked for – my family and friends, my business, my home – really did flash before my eyes. All of it gone because of my weight. Lost forever because of a few too many cheeseburgers.

Beep-beep, beep-beep... The EMT was right. My heartbeat did come back on its own without him having to shock me. Arriving at the hospital, the medical staff assumed I was having a heart attack. As I was wheeled into the Intensive Care Unit, the doctors and nurses feverishly began their work.

After a battery of tests and 11 hours in ICU, it turned out not to be a heart attack at all, but something I'd eaten. A dozen Chinese hot wings and several glasses of strong southern iced tea had caused me to have a heart arrhythmia.

There I lay, wired up and beeping, a 282-pound 45-year old-man. I suffered from asthma, acid reflux, sleep apnea, snoring, tingling limbs (an early sign of type 2 diabetes), and intense lower-back pain. I had not exercised in years and suffered from many repeated illnesses, too. I was in sad shape, to say the least.

Released from the hospital, in the week following I went to the cardiologist for a stress test. It took roughly 3 minutes into the treadmill test for me to pass out and find myself right back in the hospital again.

My cardiologist categorized me as not just obese, but "morbidly obese". I learned that I had a 51 percent body-fat content. More than half of me was pure FAT! He told me that my cholesterol and triglycerides where both over 500, which is very dangerous. My low-density lipoprotein (LDL), the "bad" cholesterol, was 198 (very high), and my high-density lipoprotein (HDL), the

1

"good" cholesterol, was 27 (low). I was told that, on an overall health scale of 1-10 – 1 being perfectly healthy and 10 being dead – my score was a 9.88. I was a walking dead man. He told me to change or write a will, because I would be dead in two years. I believed him.

Even though I was the financially successful owner of an advertising agency and had attained all the things men are typically encouraged to strive for in America – homes, cars, big-boy toys, a child in private school, etc. – at that moment, I never felt like such a complete failure. I had truly lost myself by gaining 5 pounds at a time.

What had happened to me? Where was the bright, vibrant, energetic, positive person I used to be? I came to the realization that I'd slowly made myself into an "invisible man." While I had become larger and more visible in size, my person had dwindled in my own and everyone else's eyes. Somehow I'd lost sight of myself and everything I had ever believed myself to be. It was time for the change of a lifetime.

A second chance at life had been offered to me, and I decided to make the most of it. Like many Americans, I started a diet on my own. I promptly lost 12 pounds only to encounter a weight loss plateau for the next month, and then gain 4 pounds back. I was getting the results of a typical yo-yo dieter. I was frustrated, but I wasn't going to give up that easily.

That same week, I happened to be watching TV when Oprah came on. She had Dr. Oz Mehmet on her show talking about how the human body works. I learned so much in just one show. (Thanks Oprah!) It struck me that I knew almost nothing about how my body used food. At that moment, I decided to become a learner again. I really wanted to discover how my body worked, so I started reading fitness magazines and dozens of health books. Any TV shows I could find on exercise and weight loss were TiVo'd and watched every chance I got.

With my new found momentum, I signed up for an eight-week nutrition class at the same hospital I was rushed to with my phantom heart attack. During those weeks I was inundated with knowledge. When the class was over, I was the biggest loser in the class by losing over 20 pounds in just eight weeks. I wanted and needed more.

I began researching some of the different weight-loss plans and programs. After reviewing several plans and being encouraged by a neighbor's past success, I went to my first Weight Watchers® meeting in August of 2005.

I wanted to forget the whole idea of a diet. I wanted what I have come to call a "Life-it™," an eating lifestyle that I could maintain for the rest of my life. I found some of these positive changes were in practice at Weight Watchers, so I decided to join.

At the weekly classes, I learned how to make slow and steady, small changes in my life. I began choosing proper portion sizes and better snacks. I discovered things I'd done wrong all my life and replaced them with healthier choices and better habits. Some of these choices were not simple or easy, but I knew that it was a do-or-die situation.

Motivation!

I quickly came to the realization that staying motivated was going to be of vital importance to my success. Being in advertising, I decided that I would design an ad campaign for myself. I decreed it "**yearofthetim**" and made a logo for myself. I picked a theme song, MC Hammer's "Too Legit to Quit" and put it on my iPod, and listened to it at least once a day.

Then I took a before picture and used Photoshop to give myself a new "after" physique. I printed it out and put it up on my office wall to visualize what I believed I could become.

I am the Possibility!
I can become better!
2B4L

yearofthetim

I put my logo and my slogans on paper the same size as a dollar bill in my pocket so that every time I paid for something, I'd see my logo and stay encouraged. I even embroidered the number 2 on the cuffs of my business shirts and started signing my name "Tim 2" to constantly remind myself that I had received a second chance at my life. I had a real chance to become better in every respect!

Six months into Weight Watchers, I was losing about a pound a week, which was great, but I realized I needed to do more. My Weight Watcher leader told me that, if I started an exercise program, I could lose an extra pound a week. Inspired, I did what I dreaded the most – I JOINED A GYM!

On the first day at the gym, my female dominatrix of a personal trainer put me on the treadmill and said one word, "Run." In less than five minutes, I was huddled over the trash can hurling my guts out. As a man, it was totally humiliating and very disheartening.

By her own admission, my trainer had never been overweight a single minute of her skinny little life. While I'm sure she had knowledge of how to work-out, she had absolutely no compassion and no concept of how tremendously difficult starting any workout program is for a very obese person. I dumped her after 3 days, but stuck with my goals.

Fortunately my gym had two "dark rooms," which are basically a bunch of treadmills in a room without the lights on – just a big TV showing ESPN. There, I could hide away from those I believed to be "The beautiful slender fit people." In that dark room, I could feel okay about walking on an incline of 0 at a speed of 1 mph.

I developed what I called "My 2nd Life" sound track, filled with two hours of encouraging, uplifting music. I played it in my car, when working, and while working out. It really helped me to keep a positive attitude. To the surprise of staff at the gym, in a month I was up to an incline of 2 and 2 mph. By the third month, I was up to an incline of 4 and 4 mph and was now losing up to two pounds a week.

This is what Weight Watcher's recommends as a healthy amount of weight to lose in any given week. Originally the cardiologist and Weight Watchers had set a goal weight of 210 pounds, which they believed to be a healthy weight for me. My doctor later lowered my goal to 200 pounds, because I was doing so well with my healthy progress and overall weight-loss. To help me reach this new goal, I decided to hire a really good personal trainer. He helped me get out of the dark room and into the weight room. He also introduced me to boxing to break up my workouts and move me off my weight-loss plateaus.

By the end of August 2006, 50 weeks after my hospital stay, I'd lost 68 pounds and reached my 200-pound goal weight! At my Weight Watchers meeting, my leader allowed me to share my success story with the class.

To illustrate how much weight I'd lost, I brought in a large bucket containing 70 pounds of chain. Slowly pulling it from the bucket I wrapped it around my body and locked it in place. Standing there I said "This represents my Invisible 70 Pound Fat Chain. Each link was forged by me, and I've carried it through my life for the past 27 years. I put it on one link at a time, and now I've taken it off one link at a time."

Turning the key on the lock, the chain dropped loudly, crashing into a pile on the floor. My fat chain had finally been broken. Picking up the chain and placing it in the bucket, I asked everyone in the class to come by and try to lift or carry my "old fat" chain.

Everyone was amazed at the weight of the chain. Some people couldn't lift it at all. Several could carry it only a few feet. By October, I'd lost another seven pounds and reached another goal – lifetime status with Weight Watchers.

Lifetime status means that, as long as I stay within five pounds of my goal weight, I never have to pay again to come to any Weight Watchers meeting. It's a great incentive they offer for members to keep their weight off.

Benefits

At 49 years old, and I had lost a total of 93 pounds. The best thing is that I've kept the weight off for over four-and-a-half years. When I started my weight loss journey, my percentage of body fat was 51 percent, now it's down below 14 percent. I had a 48-inch waist, which is now 33 inches for a 15-inch loss. My neck was 23 inches, now it's 16 inches.

- I ran well over 700 miles in 2007.
- I ran my first 12k in 2008, finishing in just one hour and forty-seven minutes.
- I boxed in the ring three days and work-out the other three days every week.
- I eat really amazing, healthy foods now and truly love it.
- I saved over $17,000 dollars in 2007 just by losing the weight.

Emotionally, physically, and spiritually I feel great now. I feel like a whole "visible" man again. I no longer suffer from any heart problems, back pain, acid reflux, sleep apnea, or snoring and tingling limbs. My cholesterol went from over 500 to down below 134. My triglycerides, then over 500, are now down to an astounding 81. Both are well within the healthy range.

All my health measurements (vitamins, minerals, and hormones) are textbook perfect! My doctor told me that I've cut my risk of heart attack, stroke, and diabetes by over 60 precent and added eight to fifteen years to my life. Most importantly, I'm so enthusiastic about my second chance at my life.

After 29 years of being overweight, I'll admit I never dreamed or believed I would or could have this kind of body, or this kind of peace of mind. I can truly say that my past concepts of being a successful man changed dramatically. Now I really know what being a successful man is, finding peace with yourself and being truly fit and healthy. Learning and growing every day. Giving and forgiving others. Embracing life and all the amazing opportunities it has to offer every one of us daily. I truly feel successful about my life again and about moving forward toward a brighter future. I know, deep inside, if you're honest with yourself, you really want to feel like this too.

2 Legit 2 Quit

This is why I decided to write this book exclusively for men. I know that I'm not the only man who has allowed his weight to steal his life away. My heart's desire is to help you to become a "visible man" again.

There are hundreds of books written for women that speak specifically to their needs. But there aren't many that speak realistically and honestly to a man's needs, especially to an older, overweight man's needs.

This book is filled with lessons and wisdom I've learned during my four year weight-loss journey. I know these "Chain Breakers" work. I've tested every one of them myself. They've helped and inspired me to achieve my goals, and I know that they will do the same for you.

If it's five or five hundred pounds you want or need to lose, you can do it! You need to do it, because you are important in this world, to your family and friends, and to people you haven't even met yet. I'm so fortunate that I got a second chance to believe in myself and change my life forever, to become a "visible man" again. I know you can do it too! Remember: What you believe about yourself - it all comes true! So believe the best about yourself!

Let's get started.

Tim 2 Taylor

Still lean and mean at 51,
I've learned so much about
health, weight-loss, mental,
spiritual and physical fitness.
I know this book will help you
discover how to change
your life for the better.

Two Jokers, A Large Rock And Some Bandages

My granddad and uncle were sitting on the front porch of my grandparents' tiny shack of a house outside of Atlanta, Georgia. I was a boy of 12, with very little knowledge of life. I sat on the steps and listened as my ol' granddaddy and uncle went on about playing poker. "How do you play poker anyway?" I asked. My uncle, who was a Baptist preacher, looked over at my old granddad and asked, "Do you want to teach him how to play like you were taught to play?" My granddad smiled and replied, "Yeah, I think he's old enough to learn."

My granddad looked out to the edge of the road near the mailbox and said, "See that big rock over there? Go and get it and bring it here." Excited at the opportunity of being introduced into the adult world of playing poker, I leapt to my feet and moved the boulder to the front porch as my granddad made his way into the house.

The screen door slapped closed behind my grandfather as he returned with a deck of playing cards in one hand. He also had what appeared to be a roll of bandages in the other. Reclining back into his creaking rocking chair, my granddaddy sat the bandages down on the porch in front of me. My uncle adjusted his rocker to get a better view of the goings-on.

My granddad told me to pick up the rock and hold it out in my right hand. Looking at him puzzled, I did as he had asked. Understand that this was no easy task, as it was a heavy stone. My grandfather opened the brand-new deck of cards and spoke.

"Son, the most important thing in playing poker is knowing when to get out. The first two things you've got to get out are the jokers. You'll never play a serious game of cards until you get rid of these two jokers."

Holding up the first joker he said, "This joker represents fooling yourself, and the second joker represents fooling others. In poker, as in the game of life, if you fool yourself, you'll never be a winner. If you fool others, then you'll always be a loser." I didn't quite understand what this had to do with learning poker. My mind kept drifting to the pain building in my arm from holding up the huge rock.

He continued explaining the ins and outs of suits, combinations, flushes, straights, and full houses. Under the stone's weight, my arm was burning like it was on fire. This fire was pushing out any hope I had of concentrating on the how-to's of playing the game.

My granddad encouraged me to keep the stone raised. "Come on now, don't drop that stone." I used my other hand to support my elbow in an effort to keep the stone balanced and in the air. My granddad continued instructing me on how to read a tell, bet and bluff, and how to hold out to see what is coming down the river. He talked about putting on a poker face. He clearly could see the pain building in my face and in my wobbling arm.

He asked me, "Do you want to throw the rock at my head yet?" What? I thought to myself. "Well do you?" He questioned again. To be honest, the thought did cross my mind, but I answered, "No, sir." His gravely voice questioned me again with, "Do you want to drop it?" I replied, "Oh yeah!"

" Are you absolutely sure?" He posed again.

"YES! " I yelled. "OK, then drop it." And I did. Thump to the ground it tumbled, barely missing my feet.

I started swinging my arm around like I was swatting away a swarm of bees. Feeling as if they had already stung me, the blood slowly flowed back into my numb appendage. My uncle just laughed and laughed.

I looked at my grandfather and asked, "What did holding that rock have to do with playing poker?" He said, "You see in poker as in life, it's all about judging people.

"If you judge people, you feel like they're different than you. If you judge that they've done you wrong or offended you somehow, you'll get angry. When you get angry or feel wronged, you'll pick up a rock to hit 'em with it. And you'd better pick up a big rock to make sure you knock 'em out when you throw it at their head." My uncle just laughed harder.

My grandfather continued on with his lesson. "Why didn't you throw the rock at my head when you had the chance?" he asked. "Well... I don't know. I guess because I didn't want to hurt you. You're my granddad."

"That's right. I'm your blood, and you care about me." This was his manly way of saying that I loved him and would never want to hurt him. "So did you holding that rock hurt me?"

"No sir!" I answered.

"Did it hurt your uncle here?"

"Nope."

"Who did it hurt?"

"It hurt me!" I shouted.

My old granddad went on "That's the absolute truth. When you pick up the rock of judgment, of anger or resentment, the only person that feels its weight is you. As long as you carry it around, the only one who feels the pain is you. Let me ask you this, when you dropped that stone, how'd you feel?"

I replied, "Happy and relieved!"

"Did your pain go away?"

"Yes, sir."

"Did the feeings come back to your arm and hand?"

"Yes, sir."

"Could you use your hand to pick up something else once the rock was gone?"

"Yes, sir."

"So what you need to remember is to not to ever judge somebody by the hand they're dealt in this life. They are blood just like you and me, and you've got to care about everybody exactly like you cared about me."

My ol' granddaddy shifted foward in his creaking rocking chair and reaching down he picked up the old bandages. "Here," he said, holding out the bandages and placing them into the hand that had been holding up the rock.

"What are these for?" I asked. Pausing and taking a somber breath he spoke up again.

"Always carry some bandages with you son. Because you'll never know when you'll meet someone who may be wounded and in need of a bandage. It may make a difference and could very well save their life."

He put the deck of cards back in its box and placed it in my other hand. I saw a look in his face, deep in his eyes that I'd never seen before. "I'll teach you how to play poker again some other day, okay?" He stood up and walked into the house, the screen door slapping closed behind him.

My granddad never got the chance to teach me how to play poker. He did teach me more important lessons that day. I never realized how important those lessons were until years after my granddaddy had passed away. Many years later, I was talking with uncle about that day, and he told me that on my granddad's first day at boot camp in WWII at the young age of 17, another veteran soldier had taught him to "play" poker exactly the way he'd taught me.

He said that my granddad never spoke of his time in the war except for this story and said that he had carried a roll of bandages in his pocket into every battle. On many occasions he encountered wounded men, sharing with my uncle that those rolls of bandages saved many a man's life. My uncle helped me see that the "learn how to play poker" parable was supposed to help me see that the things you have to deal with in life are the jokers, basically yourself. Your own thoughts and deeds. And the rock represents the choices and decisions we make every day. Finally, the bandages are for all the people you touch or affect in this life.

The impact of my granddad's lesson was not to be fully realized until it was I in desperate need of the bandages, laying in a hospital bed that day wondering if I was going to live or die. That day, I remembered the long forgotten story of the rock, bandage and jokers. I thought about the first thing he told me, "If you fool yourself, you'll never be a winner; and if you fool others, you'll always be a loser."

For far too long, I'd been fooling myself by thinking I could ignore my heath problems. I had to admit to myself that I hadn't dealt with the jokers in my life's deck. From that moment on I vowed to do whatever it took to stop fooling myself and others. I'd look at my decisions and change those, too. Then I looked at how my life affected others, and I wanted that to change as well. I wanted and needed to do this so I could play a very serious game, my life.

I know this is an unusual story to start my weight-loss book with. I shared this story to convince you that you have to get honest with yourself. I'll show you that you can make these changes and make your life better. Know that you can deal with the two jokers and do whatever it takes to deal them out of your own life.

If you can and will do this, I truly believe you will be successful in your weight loss effort this time and for the rest of your life. Look at the rock weighing you down, that one you might be holding onto, and see that it's keeping you from reaching for something better in your life. I strongly encourage you to let it go. Recognize that holding on to it only hurts you. Please, just drop it.

Finally, let me offer you my roll of bandages. Because, admit it or not, if you've been overweight for over a year or more, you are a wounded soul. Maybe a part of the walking wounded, but wounded just the same. This story helped save my life, and I want the chance to help you save yours.

It's my hope that after reading the chapters and the Chain Breaker tips I've included in this book, it will be a true turning point in your life.

Don't be afraid to learn something new and take that first step. Stay focused and motivated, building a never-say-quit attitude. You will become healthy, lose the weight you want, and become a healthier, happier man than you've ever been in your entire life.

Chain Breaker: Deal with the jokers in your life today. Deal with all the weight, physical, and emotional baggage that you are carrying around. Identify your personal wounds, then bandage them up and begin the healing process. Pick up a figurative bandage and carry it with you, which means take the healing that you do for yourself and start to help others while you are helping yourself. Start putting these chain breaking tips into practice and into your lifestyle from this day forward. You're in the game to win it now!

Are you an "Invisible Man?"

"Mad, I tell you! He's gone mad, stark, raving mad!" This is a famous line from the 1933 movie *The Invisible Man*. It's the story of an extremely intelligent scientist who decides to experiment on himself only to find that his experiments make him become invisible. And the side effects, or just the very fact that no one actually sees him, pushes him to complete lunacy. The only cure is a blood transfusion. Yeah, it's campy. But what a weird, fun story.

As a kid did you ever fantasize about what it would be like to be the Invisible Man? I know I did. Being able to go places and do things with complete anonymity like visiting girls' locker rooms, I thought, "How wonderful that would be!" I really never thought about the downside of invisibility.

There is an entire nation of invisible people walking among us. I know this because I used to be one of them. When I was overweight, I truly was the invisible man. With every pound I gained, I felt myself slowly fading away. The vibrant, energetic person I used to be slowly began to disappear. My true self seemed to vanish before my eyes and in the eyes of others.

We as a nation don't want to actually see obese people. I noticed this myself, as I quit looking people in the eye when I met them. I realized that people wouldn't look me in the eye either.

Sadly, we simply gloss over the fat people of this world. Yeah, sometimes people would point and laugh at me. Maybe make the occasional fat joke at my expense. But for the most part, I was invisible.

When you are overweight, you naturally want to hide, physically and emotionally. When I was looking for photos of myself during my fat years for this book, I could only find 14. I'd become the cameraman taking the pictures so that I would never have to be in them.

I looked through hundreds of photos of family gatherings, holidays, and events covering a 20 year span, and I was missing, vanished, gone. If I was captured in a photo, I was always behind someone or some larger object, hiding out.

Emotionally I'd become even more invisible. As a young man, you remember being eyed by a pretty girl across the room. You remember the swagger you had when you walked into a bar. It's at the core of manly confidence. Well, mine had left long ago, and a shallow emptiness had taken its place. No one cast a glance my way, especially not women. It was as if I ceased to matter at all. The heavier I became, the less my person seemed to mean to people, friends, and even my family. It simply made me feel like less of what a man is supposed to feel like – strong, confident, and capable.

My excess weight meant I had to shop in the big and tall man shops. I owned 27 loud flowered Hawaiian shirts, which is like a fat man's camouflage. If you have more than one of these, trust me it doesn't make you look like Magnum P.I. It means you're overweight and trying to hide the truth. I was that guy who never took his shirt off at the pool or the beach, even when I was in the water.

Outwardly, I was always smiling and jolly, a genuinely pleasant and fun guy to be around. Although I was good provider, dad, and husband, inwardly I was truly a sad, lost, broken, hurting man. A mere ghost of my former self, I'd allowed the weight to crush my sprit and hide my true heart.

When I decided to change my life by losing weight, what I really decided was that I wanted to be visible again. I wanted to matter again. I wanted people to look me in the eye. I wanted more than anything to quit being ashamed of who I'd become.

I wanted to be a fully visible man!

Mad! I tell you! He's gone mad, stark, raving mad!

Get mad! It's okay to be angry. The corporate world has experimented on you, and the side effects have made you an invisible man! They've convinced you that eating junk is totally fine. That getting fat is in the natural order of getting older. That allowing your health to crumble at 45 is just part of your modern convenience lifestyle and can be cured pharmaceutically. It is really like a science experiment gone awry. It's like being artifically kept alive so that big government, business, and medicine can steal all of your money. Let me tell you that this kind of thinking is absolute crap!

Get MAD AS HELL! The real cure is a transfusion of new blood thinking! You can eat better. You CAN lose weight and keep it off. You can become a healthy, strong, and vibrant "visible man" again.

Chain Breaker: This is a tough one. Strip down to your shorts. Take your before picture including front, back, and sides. Take a close up of your face. Print them out and keep them. Now make a vow to become a visible man again. Get mad and use your anger to drive you to do the tough things you have to do to achieve your goals and dreams.

Become a real man in 28 days.

Imagine training to run a marathon. Month after month running, and running some more. Training your body and mind for the big race. On race day you run with everything you have to within seven feet of the finish line – and then you stop!

You give up, quit, turn around, and walk away! Never crossing the finish line, never feeling the glorious victory and the flooding sense of accomplishment. Who would do that? Would you? No way, right?

Would you be surprised to know that millions of Americans do just that every day? Not in a foot race, but in the race to lose weight. It's all because we want quick results. The average person starts and tries to stay on a new diet for an average of three weeks or just 21 days.

Then, not seeing the results they imagine they should, they give up, quit trying, and go back to their old eating habits and unhealthy ways. They gain back the weight they've lost and then some. It's the old yo-yo diet syndrome.

I'm going to let you in on a secret, a powerful secret that is hidden in plain view but no one sees. If these three-week dieters had only known how close they really were to seeing truly amazing results and dramatic changes, maybe they would have stuck with it and finished the race.

What's the secret? It's our body clock, technically referred to as our circadian rhythm. We all have a body clock, not just the one that wakes you up at the same time each day, but something much larger. I'll call it your natural Bodyrhythm®. It's actually all of nature's rhythm, it's our whole body's own natural rhythm, and it's on a 28-day cycle.

Think about what happens to women every 28 days. They have a period. Ever wonder why months are around 28 days long? Think about when daylight savings time changes and it takes your body about 28 days to settle into the new time shift. Everything works on a 28-day rhythm.

Our bodies are designed to reset every 28 days. The body resets everything, all of it's body's control mechanisms. How many calories we eat and the actual weight of food we consume each day is adjusted. How much fat we store, how much sleep we get, and many millions of cells are re-programmed to better suit the current conditions we find ourselves in.

Scientist have proven that it takes around 28 consecutive days of doing something new to actually reset our bodies to accommodate these changes. So, the number of calories you consume, the energy you use, and the fat stored and burned is all based on a 28 – day cycle.

So these three-week dieters are just seven days short of seeing their bodies reset to a new way of eating or adjusting to a new workout regimen. They're just seven days away from resetting the auto calorie-fat burning thermostat of their bodies to a new healthier number.

Studies have shown that doing just about anything for 28 days in a row will reset and become a more permanent behavior. Changes in the brain and body actually do occur in that amount of time. Furthermore, if you push on for just another 28 days, these new lifestyle changes will reset and become even more tightly incorporated into the brain and body, forming a new, strong, healthy habit. As you have most likely experienced, habits are much harder to change.

Ask yourself this question: Am I a man? As a real man, can I do anything for 28 days straight without wimping out? Did you answer yes? Then take this challenge.

Chain Breaker: Whenever you start a diet, an exercise program or any change to your lifestyle, do it for 28 days non-stop! No cheating and no slacking off, period. Then man up and do it consistently for another 28 days. You will be truly amazed at the results! It's easy when you know how the body works and what the rules of nature are. So, learn to work with your natural circadian rhythm and not against it. I assure you that you'll finish the weight-loss race.

Unfolding the map while driving.

I was lost. Guys never like to admit this, especially if a woman is in the car. Fortunately, I was alone. Unfortunately, I was really lost. I reached over for the map in my glove compartment. I started unfolding the map while cruising down the interstate at 65 miles per hour. I was flipping and turning the map, trying to find the right exit and all of a sudden… BAM.

I was off the road in the median. I dropped the map. Jamming on the brakes and sliding sideways, I came to a ragged stop. Catching my breath, I thanked God that I wasn't dead or hurt. I got out and checked the car for damage (and my pants for a wet spot). After finding nothing wrong, I drove to the nearest gas station to ask for directions. I know I should have pulled over to begin with, but I was in a hurry and was already late for my business meeting.

I learned an important lesson that day. Before you start on a journey, especially to somewhere you've never been before, don't wait until you are lost to reach for a map.

Before you embark on your weight loss journey, map out your route before you get started. I can tell you from experience that you will run into traffic jams, dead ends, one-way streets, many detours, and yes, you'll run off the road and into a ditch during your weight-loss journey.

Remember when you first learned to drive a car? You went down to the Department of Motor Vehicles and got a driver's manual and a learner's permit. You spent a whole year studying that manual and begging your parents to let you take the family car down the road to the Stop and Save store for milk or other odd items. Of course, you took the long way past your girlfriend's house to get there. Upon turning 16, you were the first one in line at the DMV to take that test and get your driver's license. You invested a whole year of your life learning something because the reward was worth it – sweet freedom, fun, and females!

Well, I encourage you to a get an eating learner's permit. Set aside a year. Yes, one entire year. Mine was "The Year of the Tim" to learn about food, nutrition, exercising, and personal enrichment. From the beginning of my weight-loss journey, I was so lost. I mean, let's face it. How good of a job did our parents, our teachers, or our college professors do at teaching us how to eat, good, healthy (actually nutritious) diet? Your waistline and the numbers on the scale are your report card. Most all of us got F's.

No one shows you what the actual effects of years of continually consuming junk food has on your body and mind. Especially if you've eaten it for over 25 years like I had!

It is time to become a student again. I started by taking an eight-week nutrition class. (28 days x 2 does this sound familiar?) I can tell you that this class opened my eyes to the fact that I knew absolutely NOTHING about food! I was taught to make healthier choices, about proper portion sizes and about the hidden dangers in the foods I was eating. After losing 14 pounds during the class, I was excited about learning how to change my life forever and for the better. My reward became the actual pounds of weight I was losing. Everything I learned started to become worth my time and effort.

It was actually fun learning something new and exciting every day. I wanted and needed to know more. This was when I joined Weight Watchers. Yes, it was an hour of my time once a week, but I learned so much at those meetings. Many of the lessons were simple little things, but they really added to my understanding of eating.

I realized that my lack of knowledge had been behind the wheel of my out–of–control eating habits. It was why, for so many years, no matter how many diet journeys I went on I always ended up off the road in a ditch. You have to build a desire to learn about the foods that you are putting in your body, then map out a clear course of action.

Chain Breaker: If you're an experienced reckless eater, I can't encourage you enough to get your eating learner's permit TODAY! Find and sign up for a nutrition class. Join a Weight Watchers meeting or some other weight loss program. Make a one–year commitment to read your body's driver's manual. Begin leaning everything you can about nutrition and healthy eating. Then practice what you learn on little trips down a healthier road to a better you. It takes some time and effort, but the rewards... sweet freedom!

Eat at least 32 tablespoons of sugar every morning.

I used to get up every morning, answer nature's call, and head for the fridge to pour my first glass of soda for the day. Usually I ate at a drive-thru, but if I was going to eat what I believed to be a healthy breakfast, I'd pop a whole wheat blueberry bagel in the toaster, slather it with some cream cheese, and eat it while I was getting ready for work. I'd then wash it down with the last swig of my 16-ounce breakfast soda.

I wonder how many of you do the same thing? Do you feel sleepy after 20 minutes and wish you could crawl back into bed? When you get to work do you get another soda to get your brain in gear? By 10 a.m. are you looking for the snack machine?

This was my so-called healthy morning routine. Would you like to know what I was doing to my mind and body? I was basically putting myself into a miniature sugar coma.

You see, what I didn't realize is that everything we eat is turned into a type of sugar called glucose. It's what our bodies use for fuel. Refined foods like pastries and bagels are sort of like a high-octane jet fuel. One bagel turns into the equivalent of 17- 20 tablespoons of sugar!

Think of it this way. Your car is on empty and you stop for some gas. Your car only has a 12-gallon gas tank. Pumping in the gas – 5, 10, then 15 gallons – and the fuel starts overflowing, spilling everywhere. No matter, you just keep on pumping. 20 gallons, then 30 gallons. Finally, you stop the pump at 32 gallons. People would think you'd lost your mind! And think about how dangerous would that be. One errant spark could make the whole thing, including you, go up in flames. Anyone in his or her right mind would never do such a crazy thing. But I was doing the exact same thing to my body's fuel tank every morning.

That bagel and 12-ounce soda, once it hits your digestive system, is basically turned into the equivalent of 32 tablespoons of sugar! That's what your body actually gets. You are dumping massive amounts of refined carbohydrates, which turn into the 32 gallons of high-octane jet fuel. Try to envision that, instead of a bagel and a soda, you are shoveling tablespoon after tablespoon of sugar down every single morning.

You are not getting any real nutritional value with these kinds of meals. You're just blasting your body's blood sugar through the roof. The only thing you are increasing is

your risk of diabetes, heart disease, and stroke by upwards of 40 precent!

Realize that your body's gas tank wasn't designed to handle all this "jet fuel" at one time. It takes in all it can process (only about 10%), then pushes the rest off into fat (about 20%). After that is full, the remainder over-flows into the bloodstream (70%), causing an insulin spill that spikes you up and then crashes you down, starting what I call the "3F Domino Effect™."

The 3F's are Fast Fluctuations of Fuels that are mostly non-complex carbohydrates. You will find them in fast foods or highly refined, low-fiber foods. Upon eating these foods, your blood sugar (glucose) gets completely out of whack. Your triglycerides (blood fats) spike up three times their normal range. These major shifts within your body boost your hormones, fats, enzymes, blood pressure, and a host of other func-tions, which
cascade into reactions that topple over time into Metabolic Syndrome.

Over 25% of all Americans have Metabolic Syndrome. If you have a big belly and carry most of your weight around your middle, odds are you suffer from this syndrome.

What is Metabolic Syndrome? It exists when you have a high triglyceride level, combined with a low HDL (high-density lipoprotein cholesterol) level. Mix this with high blood pressure and a higher-than-normal fasting blood sugar level, and you've got Metabolic Syndrome. Once you have it, losing weight is virtually impossible.

The only way I've discovered to remedy this syndrome is to completely change what and more importantly when you eat. You have to re-balance the body by eliminating the massive blood sugar swings. You do this by eating more protein and complex carbs in smaller portions, several times a day (four to six meals daily). Changing to this eating schedule is a really great concept. It keeps you feeling fuller, lowers your cravings, and raises your resting metabolic rate which is essential to help you lose weight.

You need to understand that correcting Metabolic Syndrome is not a two-week process. It's a six-to eight-month process. Once you reverse its effects, the health and weight loss changes will absolutely astound you. What is the first and best step for you to take in changing this syndrome? No question about it – eat a healthy breakfast.

If you're not eating a real, nutritionally - balanced breakfast every single day (almost 50 percent of men don't eat anything at all, which is even worse for weight loss) you are cutting your ability to lose fat by a **whopping 50 percent!** The single best thing you can do to start losing weight and counter Metabolic Syndrome today is to eat a dynamically healthy breakfast.

Chain Breaker: Eat breakfast every day. NEVER miss a real, healthy breakfast. Eat at least 50% protein, 40% complex carbohydrates and 10% healthy fats. You'll see a major energy boost and dramatic weight loss. You'll be less hungry and feel fuller for a longer amount of time. Trust me you give your body what it actually needs to work properly, it will!

As I said in the opening of this book, there aren't any "you must eat this" stuff in this book. I am including what I eat for breakfast as an example of what has worked for me. What works for you may be totally different. But the important thing is that the 50-40-10 combination should be the same regardless. So here is an average breakfast for me:

• 1 - 6 oz glass of ice cold water right when I get up with my morning vitamins.

• 1 protein smoothie - mixed, 1 cup fresh fruit and 30 grams of whey protein isolate. Mix it with water, milk, or V8 fusion light juice and ice - 8oz. total.

This equals my 50% proteins (plus servings fruits and fiber).

• 1 bowl of instant oatmeal with cinnamon. This is my 40% complex carbohydrates.

Add about 6 macadamia nuts or almonds. This equals my 10% healthy fats.
This breakfast is simple, fast, properly-portioned, very nutritious, with no sugar spikes.

I know you won't eat the same thing every day for breakfast, but I challenge you to do 50-40-10 for at least 28 days in a row and see how just doing this one small thing will dramatically make a major difference in your weight loss efforts.

Just one soft drink keeps you fat.

I know the exact date that my weight problem began. It was April 23,1985.
What happened on that day that started me on my way to becoming the overweight,
out-of- shape, unhealthy, morbidly obese man I was at 45 years old?
Two words: cola wars.
This was the day the NEW version of a cola was introduced to the U.S. marketplace.

At the time I weighed 152 pounds, a weight I'd been holding at for around five years.
But my story begins with the fact that I cut my baby teeth on a soda bottle. I'm not kidding
when I say that my family drank a lot of cola. We drank it by the case, then by the liter.
As a kid, I would drink five to seven large glasses everyday. It was a very integrated part
of my life – synonymous with waking up, meal times, and going to bed from my
childhood onward.

What does this have to do with this new cola and gaining weight? Everything!
It's the single most important health factor in this entire book! I believe that no other single
food item will have as dramatic an impact on your overall health and weight loss than what
I'm about to share with you. The reason this new cola was new was because of the change
of one main ingredient. The regular cane-derived sugar was switched to high fructose
corn syrup (HFCS). Why? Because the other cola maker involved in this war had done so
earlier and realized huge cost savings over sugar, which had a very positive effect on their
bottom line. Also, because HFCS is 170 times sweeter than sugar, it sells more soda to
kids who naturally like sweeter stuff.

Within one month of switching to this new cola, I'd gained an astounding 16 pounds!
My belly became large and distended, so much that my co-workers joked that I'd

became pregnant. I wrote the sudden weight gain off as a result of stress and getting older. In reality, I now know that the HFCS began the damaging effects of Metabolic Syndrome in my body. Over the next 20 years, I gained an unbelievable 109 pounds.

Of course, I can't blame all my weight gains on my new cola habit alone. I honestly believe it contributed to my overall weight problems by 85 percent, simply because I couldn't quit drinking this stuff. I would drink an average of 2 liters every day. That's over 2,900 calories a day just from drinking cola! I was totally hooked.

Put the soda down and step away from the bottle.

I want you to listen to me. REALLY LISTEN! If you want to lose weight, STOP DRINKING SODAS TODAY! If you're drinking sodas of any kind, diet or regular, it doesn't matter. You've got to give them up.

I can hear the groans from here. I can hear the words leaving your lips right now — "I can't stop, I've got to have it to get up in the morning, and it keeps me going during the day. It's my one vice – it's my one joy in life." I've heard this from hundreds of people I've counseled on weight loss. If you ask any drug addiction specialist they'll tell you that alcoholics, smokers, and drug addicts all say the exact same words when confronted with stopping their addictions. **Face it**, If you drink more than **one** eight-ounce serving of any type of soft drink, diet or regular a day, **YOU ARE ADDICTED!**

Don't believe me? Try to stop cold turkey for a week. I double-dog-dare you! You will become mean, frustrated, and tired. You'll lose focus and concentration. You'll have cravings for soda night and day. Some of you may even get the shakes and suffer from horrible headaches. All are classic signs of addiction withdraw or what I refer to as the DTs a sort of detoxing. It's your body's way of trying to heal itself from the damaging things you've put into it.

The real basics

Let me share with you some of the bare basics about HFCS and artificial sweeteners. Both trick your body into thinking it has received a large amount of high-octane jet fuel to burn in its engines. The problem is that HFCS can't burn. Your body wasn't designed to process this stuff. It turns this HFCS to fat stores almost instantaneously. HFCS and artificial sweeteners confuse the chemical messages your body uses to signal hunger and fullness, further confounding your weight-loss efforts.

HFCS also causes a bacteria problem. Our bodies can have over 500 types of bacteria in our upper and lower intestines. They form a shared relationship with the human digestive system. Many of these bacteria are good, actually consuming fats in our diet, and break them down for use in our bodies. Other types of bacteria break down foods and turn them into fats. These fat-making bacteria in your intestines consume HFCS, which causes them to rapidly multiply overtaking the good bacteria that eats fats in your GI tract. This bacteria growth throws your intestinal flora and fauna completely out of balance. In effect, it blocks the nutrient receptors in you upper and lower GI tract.

This prohibits your body from getting many of the nutrients it needs. And in turn, it triggers you to feel the need to eat more, which you end up doing over and over again. All you get from drinking soda is more body fat and more fat-making bacteria.

Getting to the bottom of things

The adverse health effects of HFCS are staggering. Worldwide obesity has sky-rocketed with its use, especially in the United States. Before 1985, diabetes in our society had been holding at a fairly constant level. But from 1986 forward, the number of individuals being diagnosed with diabetes has exploded. What changed in the U.S. to cause this diabetic explosion? Studies have repeatedly pointed to just one culprit – the introduction and wide-spread use of HFCS in the soft drink and food industries.

The really bad news is that HFCS has permeated virtually every processed food we consume. It's become a multi-billion-dollar industry. It affects the profits of thousands of major corporations, farmers, giant food makers, the soft drink industry, doctors, and pharmaceutical companies worldwide.

Why do you think fast food restaurants offer free refills on soft drinks? Do you think it's because they like you? HA! They know it will keep you eating more fast food, making them rich and you fat! Do you think these major corporations care if this stuff is damaging the lives of you and your kids or that it's killing you slowly? Absolutely not! You'll get more concessions from the cigarette makers. At least they tell you their products will eventually kill you.

The Corn Refiners Association has even created a "SweetSuprise" pro-HFCS website promoting HFCS as a preemptive strike to try and counter all the bad publicity. This is exactly like the false and misleading marketing that the tobacco industry did in the 50s and 60s! These corporations are only concerned with one thing, their own profits!

Be a loser and a winner!

If you give this stuff up, you'll lose weight as a result faster than from anything else in this book. As much as 10 pounds or more in three weeks, without a doubt. Once I kicked the cola monkey off my back, I lost more than 13 pounds by doing nothing more than giving up soft drinks.

Vowing never to touch the stuff again, I've been almost 5 years clean – lighter and healthier because of it. I try at every turn to avoid any HFCS and artifical sweeteners by checking the ingredient labels on almost everything I eat or drink.

The wealth of worldwide independent research studies I've seen have all concluded that HFCS is just not good for your health, even in small amounts. Don't just take my word for it, I encourage you to learn more about HFCS and artificial sweeteners through your own research. Learn about the negative effects they have on your weight and overall health. Once you do, I'm sure you'll easily give them up just as I have, for good and forever.

Chain Breaker: Stop drinking colas. Don't go cold turkey. Start by cutting back. I used *Diet Snapple Peach Tea*. Yes, I know it has artifical sweetener in it, but you have to start somewhere to break the chain, and I needed it for caffeine replacement.

Then wean yourself slowly off this by adding water or more ice over a 4 week period. Start substituting fresh fruit juices (there are dozens to choose from) and water. I often used fruit juices to naturally flavor my water.

Check the labels of everything you eat and drink, because HFCS and artifical sweeteners are everywhere. The more you can keep them out of your body, the better off you'll be in the long run. Doing just this one thing will allow your taste buds to become less accustomed to sweet taste and reduce your cravings for sweets. It will also allow the good bacteria a chance to regain a balance in your GI tract, giving you a fighting chance in your weight loss efforts. I recommend adding a probiotic supplement to your daily routine to aid in the fostering of good bacteria in your GI tract. I use a product called *Acidophilus Pearls* and it can be purchased online or at any health food store.

Learn all the code names for surgars so you can recognize and avoid them. Here is just a small sample of the many deceptive names of sugars and substitutes: Sucrose, Dextrose, Corn syrup, Corn starch, HFCS, Turbinado, Sorbitol, Mannitol, Xylitol, Fructose, Lactose, Maltose. Non-nutritive sweeteners: Saccharin, Aspartame, Sucralose. Avoid them like the plague! Then watch the first 10+ pounds just melt off effortlessly.

It's not zombies eating your brain.

Rising from the dead. Scary, slime-covered zombies roam through the city, mindlessly eating your brains. *Night of the Living Dead* was a great date movie. It always frightened your girlfriend, getting her to snuggle up close for your protection. While this movie was a great work of fiction, hopefully you're not among the living dead.

When I say "living dead," I'm speaking of the mindlessly eating part of being a zombie. If you really examine how you eat, I think you'll discover that it's not far from a fictional story for most of us.

As young guys, we were always on the go. It seemed like I was always in a drive-through line or with my buddies at a fast food hangout... eating junk. Once I hit middle-age, I kept eating like I did when I was young. I was cooking ribs and munching chips with dips during the big game. Then I'd go out and party after a win which always included food. Eating was a vital part of everything we did. Consuming pastries in the morning, hot wings at lunch, pizza, ice cream, chips, and candy while watching TV at night. It wasn't that I was really all that hungry; it was just a pattern I'd fallen into. I call it "Zombie Eating®."

It's the mindless consumption of food and drink just to have something to do while watching or enjoying something else. Getting together with friends at a sporting event or just sitting around watching TV, I was always zombie eating. The real horror of this tale is the terrible types of food I consumed. Everything was high in sodium and fats. Really high fat fried chicken, burgers, fries and onion rings, chips and cheese dips, pies and ice creams for desert. Zombie eating combined with no exercise made me what is laughingly referred to as "a heart attack waiting to happen."

Once, as part of a life insurance physical, the nurse needed to do a blood test to check my cholesterol levels. She pricked my finger to get a drop of blood, and I swear that a grease stain spread out on the pad where the blood droplet landed. The nurse said she'd never seen that happen before. My cholesterol couldn't be registered with that test as it was off the scales! It was later tested to be over 500!

My cardiologist told me "Mr. Taylor, you are among the walking dead." I wasn't happy, and if you are a zombie eater you shouldn't be happy either. Here are some questions you need to ask yourself about eating habits and knowledge of cholesterol:

Part One - Do I zombie eat? Do I mindlessly eat and drink things that pass as food, without knowing how many calories I'm consuming at a given sitting? Do I mindlessly munch on snacks at night while watching TV or a movie? Do I pile food up on my plate (sometimes two plates) so I won't miss anything? Do I eat at buffets a lot?

Part Two - Do I know anything about cholesterol in general? What are HDL and LDL? Which is the good and which is the bad cholesterol? What should my levels of each be for my height and age? Do I know how to raise the good and lower the bad naturally, without using drugs? Do I know the consequences of not knowing the answers to these questions?

Did you answer no to any of these questions? If you answered yes to at least one question in part one and no to at least one question in part two, odds are you're among the "walking dead" too.

Chain Breaker: Brains. I need brains! Use your noggin! Write down everything you eat and drink for at least a week. Beside each entry write down your hunger level, ranked from 1 (starving) to 10 (stuffed). Before you eat anything – stop and think first.
Ask yourself these 7 questions: 1. Am I really hungry? 2. Is this just social eating?
3. How much am I eating? 4. How long has it been since I last ate a snack or a meal?
5. How nutritious is the food I'm about to eat? 6. How much fat and sodium does it contain? 7. Can I find anything healthier right now to satisfy my hunger?
Catch yourself whenever you might be zombie eating and stop giving in to it.
Start using your brain before you start filling your belly!

Then go to your doctor and get your cholesterol tested. Don't eat or drink anything from midnight the night before and go as early the next day as possible. Get the results and determine to make them better.

Emotions are totally edible.

As guys, we think we aren't particularly emotional. After all we don't tear up at a sappy commercial with cute puppies or at some chick flick. We're just not made that way. We internalize our feelings. We keep our emotions in check. After all, we are men... right? We think of emotions in terms like, "Real men don't cry."

It's just that simple. What we don't think about is why do we have emotions, and what causes an emotional response? Everyone knows that there are both positive and negative emotions. How many emotions do you think we as humans experience?

Would you be surprised to know that scientists have identified 56 positive and 63 negative emotions? That's 119 emotions in total! Scientist have also identified that each emotion we experience triggers an emotional response. That automatic response is based largely on how we were raised. The word "trigger" is an interesting way to describe what happens to us as human beings. As guys, we know that when you pull a trigger there's usually a bang and a bullet that hits a target. That's really very close to what happens with our emotions and overeating or what is called "emotional eating."

I discovered that I was an emotional eater. I would have never in a million years guessed that I was. I've since learned that 30% of obese people are emotional eaters, and that number breaks evenly at 15% women and 15% men. So emotions and their triggers have no regard for gender.

Scientists have also found that negative emotions have a significantly stronger effect and generate a much higher need to console ourselves with "comfort" foods. These negative emotions trigger men's bodies to convert calories to fat much faster than in women. It appears that as men we try to control our emotions. We tend to "eat them" as a way to deal with these negative emotions and make ourselves feel better.

I tracked my emotional status for 28 days. I did it every single time I ate anything.

What I discovered was that almost all of my emotions when I ate were negative. I felt tired, angry, ignored, lonely, anxious, exhausted, overwhelmed, depressed, indifferent, bored, sad, and stressed. I had 13 of the 63 negative emotions that kept popping up over and over again, before or while I was eating. I learned that my emotions played a much greater role in my life than just not crying at a chick flick.

I began to see that these emotions were triggering a want to eat as a way to deal with how I was feeling. This eye-opening experience (EOE™) forced me to look at the underlying causes of my negative emotions. I had to learn, with the help of a psychologist and therapist, to deal with what was going on in my head and my heart. This, in turn, helped me deal with what I was putting in my mouth. It was hard to admit that I actually have emotions because, as men, we don't think about them... ever.

I was never taught how to deal with emotions that I didn't realize I was having or even knew existed. I can honestly tell you that getting a handle on these emotions and working through my emotional issues has played a significant role in my weight-loss success. I learned that overeating wasn't my real problem. I realized that overeating was how I was coping with most of my problems, and that this coping mechanism was killing me. I discovered my core underlying problems and dealt with these issues head-on, instead of just trying to just cope with them. I know you can do it, too.

Finding your Food Wound™

Almost every overweight person I've come in contact with has had what I call a "Food Wound™." A Food Wound marks a time or a place in your life in which you experienced a great pain, such as on-going bullying, harassment or teasing as a child. Actual sexual abuse, physical or mental neglect. Maybe the loss of a parent or loved one, or a divorce. Whatever it might be, the wound is something that has had a strong emotional effect on you on a powerful subconscious level. This pain is real – it's an open emotional wound and, undoubtedly, you've covered that Food Wound with food and lots of it. Let me encourage you to go back, find your Food Wound, and heal it in your head and in your heart. Learn to stop covering up the pain with food.

Chain Breaker: While you are tracking your daily eating and drinking habits, look at the emotions list (in the back of the book) and find the emotions you are feeling when you start to feel hungry. Check the list to see if you're having a negative or positive emotion. If you discover you are an emotional eater, find a professional to help you learn how to really deal with these issues.

Thieves are in your house. Get out NOW!

Whole grain, 0 trans-fat per serving, high in fiber, all-natural, low-fat, reduced-calorie, fat-free, healthy 100-calorie snack packs. All of these things have one thing in common. Can you guess what it is? It's a magician's best friend. It's misdirection.

It is the subtle art of making you see what you want to see and not notice the sleight-of-hand work behind the illusion. We go to a theater to see a magic show, as amazed viewers, we ooh and ahh at their feats of prestidigitation. We suspend our belief in the impossible and believe what we see.

We see it. We hear it, so we want to believe it. But when we leave the theater, we don't think about the fact that we've been fooled or tricked. We just say, "How'd they do that?" Have you ever seen an illusion and then been shown how the magician performs the trick? You say to yourself, "Oh my gosh, it was so simple. How was it that I didn't see that?"

Once you've seen through the trickery of the illusion, the trick will never work on you again... will it? Well, right here, right now I'm going to expose a couple of the food industry's best magic tricks. Once you've seen how the illusions work, you'll never be fooled again.

Now I'm no magician, but I am uniquely qualified to expose the trickery due to my work as an advertising and marketing professional. I've been in the ad game for more than 30 years and, believe me, I've seen all the tricks.

Let's start with the obvious one first. The so called "healthy" words, like whole grain, natural, fresh, low, and reduced-calorie. I want you to see how these healthy words are like a cow in the field. The cow eats grass, chews, walks around, and drops a loaf of field dough, all hot and steamy. Now let's use our healthy words to describe her handy work. Is the turd "whole grain"? Yep. Is it "natural"? Yep. Is it "fresh"? Yep. Is it "low"? Well it's on the ground, so yes. Is it "reduced calorie"? It does have less calories then the original grass had so... yes, again. So would you eat the hot steamy loaf of field dough?

It's got all the right healthy words associated with it, so why not? Why? Because you know it's all bullshit! That is what 99% of all healthy packaging is, misdirection. It's a way to get you to not see the bullshit for what it is. Don't be fooled, it's all just deceptive sleight of hand.

Now let us look at the trickery involved in portion sizing. Let me tell you, I used to love Snickers candy bars. My friends used to call me the "Snickers Man" because I ate one or more almost every day. Now a regular size bar is, well, a regular size, right? You'd eat the whole thing and not think anything of it. Maybe wash it down with a bottle of cola as a quick snack. But the "magic" is in the measuring.

See if you'd look on the back of the wrapper for that so-called nutrition label and look right at the top you'll see the serving size. Guess what the serving size of a regular bar is. It's TWO servings! And that bottle of cola? It's TWO-AND-A-HALF servings!

Yep, you just consumed over two times the amount of empty calories than you thought you had, and it all turns to FAT! You would have to RUN on a treadmill for over 2.5 hours non-stop to burn off those calories. These two simple tricks are the core of the food industry's huge bag of illusions.

Understand and see these companies for who and what they are. They are not just magicians, they are "thieves" that are in your house right now. They're in your pantry and fridge. They are stealing your health from right under your nose, and they are raking in huge profits out of your wallet while doing it. Now you've seen how the tricks work, don't buy into their "healthy" packaging anymore.

Chain Breaker: Start food shopping for yourself. Look at the nutritional information and see past the magical wording. Look at labels to see the truth. See what they are hiding from you: high sugars, high sodium, mislabeled fats, false portion sizes, and dozens of unhealthy additives. Find better, more nutritious choices and buy them instead. Put low-calorie, high-fiber fruits and vegetables in place of fake food in your home. Know proper portions. Eat more live stuff, organic local produce if at all possible, and your resulting weight loss won't be just an illusion.

I was almost a woman. Are you?

What makes a man a man? There are, of course, many things that make a man. But chemically, what is it that determines the difference between men and women? Besides the extra chromosomes, it comes down to two powerful hormones... estrogen for women and testosterone for men. Each sex has a combination of both, but the balance is dramatically different. For a 20-year-old male, the normal level of free testosterone is between 720mg to 1100mg. For a woman 40mg to 97mg of testosterone is a normal range.

Hormones are the powerhouses of the body. The things they affect and control is astoundingly important. Your sex drive, energy levels, muscle mass, fat burning and storage, erectile function, moods and depression, mental acuity, and even digestion.

When women hit menopause, their estrogen levels can drop dramatically. This is why many women have estrogen replacement therapy to counter the negative effects of loss of estrogen in their bodies. Did you know that after the age of 35, men can experience the same type of hormone loss?

We can actually lose testosterone from our bodies. This is called andropause. I had never heard this word and had no idea that it happens to men. I also had no clue of the effects or the damage that could occur from having a low testosterone level.

How did I discover that I had andropause? After I had lost most of my excess weight, I was a healthy 195 pounds. I'd been exercising with my trainers for almost eight months. Although I was losing weight, I wasn't putting on any muscle. Frustrated with my lack of results, my trainer recommended that I seek medical advice.

So I went to doctor after doctor trying to find out what was going on with my body and I got nowhere fast. Every one of the doctors I saw were male. You would think that they would have some experience with what was happening to me, but they knew absolutely nothing! Not one of them ever thought to test my estrogen and testosterone levels. This is a sad commentary on the state of preventive health care in America.

This is why I strongly recommend that you keep searching for a good doctor who believes in a natural response to ailments and who specializes in men's health issues. I've found that holistic medical doctors and physicians with training in Eastern medicines are more sensitive to these issues. Frustrated, I happened to mention my problems in a conversation with my accountant. He told me about an amazing doctor he'd discovered, Dr. Michelle Mendez D.O., and of all things she's a woman.

She had tested him and determined that he had all the signs of andropause. When he described the symptoms he'd been experiencing, I thought that he was reading from a list of my symptoms. I made an appointment to see her that day. She spent two hours listening to my problems. Then she tested my free testosterone, estrogen, vitamin, and mineral levels. The results were shocking. My testosterone level was 111mg, (normal is between 720mg to 1100mg.) I was just 14mg away from having the same testosterone levels as a healthy woman! And my estrogen levels were extremely high, too.

What I'd learned is why all those guys you see on those biggest weight-loss shows are always crying and emotional, angry and exhausted. I discovered that when you've carried a lot of weight, especially around your waist, for many years – or have metabolic syndrome your body starts making more estrogen and storing within your fat cells. Then that fat produces even more estrogen.

When you start burning your fat stores, it dumps all that stored estrogen into your bloodstream. This in turn dramatically lowers your already plummeting testosterone levels. This hinders your weight-loss efforts and so much more.

If you are frequently sad, grumpy, moody or depressed, lacking energy, have a decreased sex drive, erectile dysfunction, loss of muscle mass, or can't seem to add muscle, or are experiencing strength and endurance problems, then it's possible that the cause of all of your problems is low testosterone levels. If you notice any of these symptoms while losing weight or if you're over 40, get a simple blood test to check your testosterone and estrogen levels. Man to man, you'll be glad you did.

Two Important Warnings:

1. I'm a firm and ardent believer in **never** using any kind of drugs unless absolutely necessary. Don't think that this doctor-prescribed and closely monitored testosterone replacement therapy in any way resembles the use or abuse of anabolic steroids. It in no way resembles the extremely high doses of testosterone used by some sport figures or bodybuilders. This is a very, very low-dose replacement therapy (only 1% solution) designed to restore your body's own natural levels of testosterone.

Any medication should only be taken under the guidance of a physician. Don't fall for these muscle magazine ads or fly-by-night hormone treatment clinics. If they don't have an on-site, full time, licensed physician who will monitor you at least monthly, **RUN** the other way.

Understand the abuse of anabolic steroids is bad, very dangerous, and almost always illegal. Never buy any drugs or anabolic steroids over the Internet or from a guy at the gym. They may promise is quick and amazing results, but all they deliver is death.

Stay Clean! It's the only true way to get real, rewarding, and lasting results, without risking the good health you are working so hard to achieve.

2. Everything you put into your body affects your body. I've had some quirky side effects from the testosterone. Weird things like songs getting stuck in my head continually and some strange dreams at night. Once, as a test, my doctor switched manufacturers of the testosterone, and the new stuff gave me huge body acne on my chest and back. Switching back to the original manufacturer's formula resolved this problem.

I've had some machismo issues too, like every so often getting disproportionately angry or pissed off over trivial things, but nothing ever out of my control. I've had many more positive effects that more than out weigh any of these slight unusual side effects.

I tell you this so that you'll ask your doctor about how it might affect you. Also let them know that you'll probably be taking other vitamins and supplements.

Chain Breaker: Watch for the symptoms of having a low testosterone level, such as a general tiredness, easily fatigued, consistently low sex drive, moodiness, and an inability to sleep well. Get your T-level checked by a doctor, then start replacement therapy if necessary. Monitor your T-levels with your doctor with a simple blood test at least every 3 months. If you've ever had prostrate or heart problems, be sure to discuss these issue with your doctor before you start taking any testosterone replacement therapy.

Believe me you'll, be feeling like a real man again in no time.

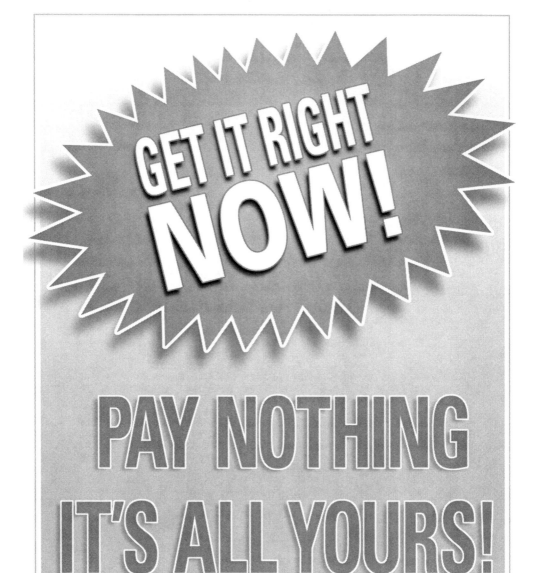

(Untill you turn 45, then the full amount is due with interest. At a rate of 50% increased chance of death.)

Buy it now with no payments for 12 years.

We've all heard the furniture commercials that shout, "Get a whole room of furniture now, interest-free. You pay nothing for two whole years!" You hustle down and sign the papers and bingo, you've got a beautiful room of furniture to rest your ass on.

It's all fine and dandy until two years down the road when the bill comes due. And in the fine print (that you failed to read) it states that the whole amount is due right now or you can make monthly payments with an interest rate of 37.9%. Shock! You look at your once beautiful furniture, all broken down, covered with stains and rips. You then realize that you've made a terrible mistake. Now you've got to pay a very high price, and there is no way out. There is just one word for it, painful.

The cost of life is pain. The real down-to-the-bone reason that 99% of people don't exercise is pain or the perception thereof. Working out is perceived to be not easy. Walking, jogging, running, lifting weights, doing an active sport or a class causes you to hurt some, and it's hard. Oh boo-hoo... you big cry baby!

Hey, don't feel like I'm picking on you, I used to whine and complain about exercising like a wussy too. I learned to man-up and embraced the struggle.

If you don't currently exercise, you're fooling yourself into thinking, "Hey I'm not having any problems (i.e. pain) with this lifestyle. I'm good!" In reality, it's just like buying that furniture. You can sit on your ass for awhile, but someday soon you will absolutely have to pay your bill with interest. Believe me, you'll have to pay a very high price for your unhealthy lifestyle.

In America, we are conditioned to live the easiest life possible and worry about paying for it tomorrow. When it comes to your health, we eat nothing but junk – thousands of chemically created artificial calories every day, we never exercise, and we get fatter and unhealthier because of it. Let me tell you with all assurance that the cost if you don't exercise will be great and inescapable 12 years from now.

Working out will never hurt like the pain of a finger prick three times a day and a needle injection every day for the rest your life when you develop diabetes. Then losing the ability to eat what you want, when you want. And don't forget the loss of feeling in your limbs due to the nerve damage.

The pain payments only increase when you lose your eyesight as diabetes continues its ravaging path through your body. Next, your toes and fingers will have to be amputated and then part of your leg. I've witnessed it firsthand in my family, and this pain price is terrifyingly costly. By the time you've realized the mistakes you've made with an unhealthy lifestyle, it will be too late to change. The debt is due in full. Your pain debt is too great and the only way out of it, unfortunately, is complete bankruptcy and the ultimate pain – death.

What I've learned on my weight-loss journey is that you have to pay with sweat cash for your health! Pay for your healthier lifestyle with a little sweat cash every day, and you'll be banking the interest of a longer, less painful life as you get older.

If you are not exercising now, then undoubtedly you will have some aches, pains, and sore muscles once you begin an exercise program. Maybe even some bruises or injuries. And, if you push yourself too hard, you will be sore the next day for sure. Guess what? Your body actually adjusts to pain. Soon, you won't be as sore and your body will adapt and get stronger. It just takes a little time.

You will be amazed at what you'll be able to do and achieve painlessly within just a few short months. This is a very low price to pay for a healthier, more active, lighter body weight and a longer, more rewarding life.

Chain Breaker: Embrace the struggle and change it to a strength! Make payments with low-cost pain cash now. Manage your aches and pains naturally, get a massage (I get one twice a month), soak in a hot tub (I do it almost daily), put some ice on it (all the friggin time). Don't put off starting to exercise anymore. Get your doctor's approval and start an exercise routine today! The return on your investment will be the greatest wealth you'll ever accumulate here on earth – a longer healthier life.

Seeing the ghosts in the night.

In his book *A Christmas Carol,* Charles Dickens gave us quite possibly the best illustration of human nature I've ever come across. Undoubtedly, you've heard the story told, read the book, or seen an adaptation of it at the movies. I've even seen it performed on stage several times. But, trust me, you've never really seen it!

Be prepared for another EOE™ here.

When the ghost of Christmas present arrives on the scene, he appears happy, jolly, and large. He's well-groomed, dressed in ermine and red velvet, carrying a great horn of plenty in his arm and a wreath of light about his head.

He's speaking to Scrooge in the dark, cold night under a bridge about his personal responsibility to society at large. After overhearing the conversation of a homeless, out-of-work, destitute father and his sorrow-filled, yet hopeful wife, the ghost does something to shock Scrooge into opening his eyes. Remember when the ghost opens his robe (I call it a cloak) and hidden underneath are two emaciated children – he called out to Scrooge and said, "Look upon them! Their names are Hunger (Want) and Ignorance." So terrible was the very sight of them that Scrooge gasped, recoiled, and quickly looked away. He begged the ghost to cover them up, screaming, "I don't want to see them, hide them from my sight." Out of sight out of mind, right? The good ghost quickly complies with Scrooge's pleas. But the ghost said these words "They are always with you." Wow! Always with us and brother, let me tell you that this is the absolute truth.

That's the way we are as men today, all are happy and jolly and large on the outside, well-clothed, wreaths of lights upon our heads, horns of plenty in our hands. But we never want to look underneath the cloak, especially our own, to see what's underneath.

You need to see that hunger and ignorance are always with you, every day of your life.

In my life, I had the cloak pulled back and was forced to look at what was underneath (in the back of an ambulance) just as Scrooge did. It was revealed before me. I didn't want to look at it, but I was forced to see it.

Looking back now, this was one of the best things that ever happened to me. I had to look at the two terrors in the face. Here is your EOE eye-opening-experience.

Yes, I looked, and I quickly tried to cover them back up again. I didn't want to see them, and I certainly didn't want anyone else to see them. But their memory would not leave my mind. Etched indelibly was the sight of the two. This was it. The tap root, the boiled down, hard-core reality of the causes of my true life's pain.

What do you mean, Tim? How can hunger and ignorance be the cause of your weight problems? Your so-called life's problem?

Believe me I had a hunger. Not for food or nourishment per se, but a hunger for more. What was that more? It was more meaning to my life here on this earth. A need for more love, more kindness, more giving, more peace, more hope. It was this basic human hunger I had too long ignored, buried and cloaked over, in my life.

As men, we don't want to admit that we have wants and needs of an emotional and spiritual nature. We've been deceived into believing that it's not manly. Believe me, I feel more manly and have become a much stronger man because of my examination into these real hunger issues.

Speaking to this hunger, I'm sure Dickens meant to illustrate the actual starvation that was all around him in his time. Actually, that's what I hope to illustrate to you, too. I've seen that the vast majority of people in this world are still starving today, but for a different kind of nourishment. They are starving for emotional and spiritual sustenance. It's a very basic, real need to simply matter in this world. I was an overweight, starving man myself. I believe that if you're honest with yourself, you'll discover that you have this deep-seated hunger residing within you, too.

I had an Ignorance in my life also, true ignorance of what I had allowed others to do to me in my lifetime. I realized my ignorance about how my mind, body, and sprit all interact and function together as one in harmony, they make a life really worth living. I never realize that I already possessed the power within myself to change anything in my life. That I'd always had the potential to become more yet hadn't acted upon it.

I became aware of my overwhelming ignorance about my own health, food, and nutrition and how I'd been eating to keep the cloak over my own Hunger and Ignorance for many years.

Finally, I came to the realization that I should have been trying to help others to change their lives for the better throughout my whole life. In this revelation, I made the biggest change of all — I had a change of heart. I know you can too.

Chain Breaker: Look under your own cloak at the ghosts hilding just below the surface. Actually see the Hunger and Ignorance that assuredly exist in your life. Just like old Scrooge you might be frightened at first. That's a natural response, you can work through it. Take out a piece of paper and write the Hunger and Ignorance you find in your life down. line by line. Take the time to really see it. Resolve in your mind to do whatever it takes to permanently change this Hunger and Ignorance. Don't be afraid to ask for help or seek professional help to clarify this area of your life. I firmly believe if I had not dealt with my ghost, I would not have been successful in my weigh-loss efforts. Trust me, be just like Ebenezer... have a change of heart for the rest of your healthier life.

Learn how to tie knots and write a will.

Remember high school gym class? Specifically, climbing the rope? Remember how difficult climbing that rope was, both going up and coming down? When you were on that rope your best friend was the knots. You know, that big knot tied every so often. It gave you something to reach for as you were climbing up and a place to hold on to when you were coming down. It was a focus point and a resting place when you were exhausted.

You'll need these knots in this weight-loss climb, too. Losing weight and keeping it off is always tough. You're going to be surprised how the small things can make a huge difference, just like the knots in the rope.

To help you in your fitness/weight-loss journey, all you'll need is to do is drop the "k" in knots. The kind of knots you'll need are nots. "I'm **not** going to quit this time." "I'm **not** going to eat that doughnut." "I'm **not** putting anymore junk into my body." Just like the knots in the rope, you'll find that when your new lifestyle is hanging by a thread, these nots will save you and keep you from falling.

Add these nots into your daily routine. When you're tempted to let go, you'll remember to tie some nots into your rope to hang on to. More importantly you'll use them to keep moving upward! I find myself saying "I'm not" going to do something detrimental to my goals, lifestyle, or to sabotage my weight-loss efforts at least five to ten times every day.

As men, we have been conditioned to never deny ourselves. We don't like to say "no" or "not" to anyone (except maybe our kids), but especially not to ourselves.

Learning to add nots to your internal conversation will absolutely help you stay on your way to achieving your goals.

Let's move on to writing a will. I'm not talking about a will to be read to your loved ones after you've shed your mortal coil. I'm talking about writing "I wills."

Even more importantly than putting nots into your lifestyle, adding wills to your internal and external conversations is essential. It is one of the most powerful activators in making positive changes to your lifestyle. Saying it out loud, "I will" (go on, say it now) takes on a real power. Writing it down makes the intangible idea of a commitment tangible, even transcendent, somehow.

It actually becomes more real. It's something you can see and touch. This realness makes all the difference. "I **will** exercise today." "I **will** control how much and what I eat." "I **will** make myself better today." "I **will** laugh more today." You need to learn how to make nots and wills a simple part of your new lifestyle.

Chain Breaker: Write down all the things you are **not** going to do anymore. I mean everything you can think of that is holding you back. Anything that could be keeping you from becoming what you want to become. Start every sentence with, "I'm NOT."

Then write down all the things you **will** do to make your goals a reality. Start every sentence with, "I WILL."

Print out at least 3 copies of each. Keep one copy in your bathroom, one copy at the office, one copy in your car. Read it out loud every day and you'll start feeling the change. I keep one by my bed and read it every night and every morning when I get up.

It really helps to work these ideas into part of your subconscious thinking. Remember that just reading won't change anything. You must turn these thoughts into actions in your life to see them become a reality.

Sinbad's danger-filled journey.

Ever watch one of those old Sinbad movies on late-night TV? You know, the ones with the cheesy stop-motion fighting skeletons and the lizards made to look like giant dinosaurs? Those movies were great fun to watch as a kid. You could imagine setting out on a grand adventure to recover an ancient relic or rescue a kidnapped voluptuous maiden. Undoubtedly, Sinbad and his crew would encounter perilous and grave dangers on their journeys: one-eyed Cyclops, multi-headed hydras, lusty singing sirens, angry giants, and unscrupulous wizards. There was a new horrible danger jumping out at every turn. Somehow, by hook or by crook, Sinbad defeated or vanquished all of them. He recovered the golden fleece, rescues the hot chick, then sails off into the sunset victorious. Huzzah!

I can tell you that your weight-loss grand adventure will be just as perilous and fraught with dangers lurking around every bend. And, unless you are alert and ever diligent, unless you bring all of your intelligence and heart to the fight, these dangers can and will destroy you.

I discovered along my journey that the real key to weight loss isn't just what you put into you mouth. It's more about what you put into your head. How you act and react in the moment. How you trust your own heart. This is the true hero's journey.

Sinbad's monstrous encounters gave him the opportunity to test his mettle in real-world battles. Would he have the smarts, determination, courage, and stamina to overcome and win? Could he see through the tricks and temptations while keeping his ship on course through stormy seas? I don't know about you, but as a man, I love a good challenge and a chance to prove the mettle that I'm made of. I think challenge is written deep in a man's DNA.

Let me warn you about some of the dangers you are more than likely going to encounter along your grand weight-loss adventure.

Inner Demons – These are the Medusa's that haunt you with questioning doubts, such as I've never been able to lose weight. I won't stick with this. I'll gain it all back and then some. I can't do this. It's going to be too hard. I don't have the time. I'll never achieve this. I'll be hungry all the time. And so many more. Don't let this multi-headed hydra
defeat you. Cut them off at the head. Replace negative thoughts with the positive affirmations "I can" and "I will." Do it every time you hear yourself utter any of these phrases. The earlier you slay this monster the better.

External Jealousy – These are family members, friends, and co-workers who see you're doing something positive with your life that they won't do for themselves. They will turn on you and tempt you to go off of your plans. They might seem to be encouraging, but underneath they don't want you to succeed. It's unsettling and causes insecurities in others when they see you taking control of your life when they have not done the same. Don't let these sirens sway you off course. Find new friends or encourage your family and friends to join you in your journey. Stay strong!

Horrible Hormones – When you start changing from your bad eating and exercising habits to your new healthy lifestyle, your body responds in strange ways. My estrogen levels shot through the roof, and my testosterone levels plummeted. When they get out of balance, so does everything in your body. You can get emotional, angry, depressed, confused, and forgetful. Don't let these angry giants take you down. Outsmart them. Get professional help from your doctor to bring down this giant Cyclops.

Divine Assistance

I encountered all of these monsters and many more on my journey. I realized early on that I needed help to overcome these many dangers. So I sought it out. I enlisted the help of a psychologist, nutritionist, sports medicine doctor, therapist, several personal trainers, and spiritual advisors. I also took many classes and read hundreds of books and magazines.

I don't feel embarrassed or ashamed in any way for turning to these advisors for help. There is nothing unmanly about asking for help. Every football player has a coach. Every soldier has a platoon leader and the guys in his squad covering his back.

I can tell you truthfully that I couldn't have achieved my goals nor maintained my results without their support, guidance, insights, and prayers. Below is one of my favorite quotes, which I discovered on my journey and would like to share with you. I found it to be very true and helpful.

One must be whole and ready.
For the fight will come.
And he who has the skills and the wisdom
will be ready for the day. Ready to fight back.
And the fight is usually with one's self.
Ancient Samurai Saying

What I believe this ancient saying was trying to convey is that, whatever we encounter in our daily life, the struggle is really within ourselves in the choices we make, how prepared we are to make the correct choices, and choosing to act on them appropriately. Just as the Samurai had to be prepared and ever ready to fight off any threat or personal attack, so should you make yourself as whole and as ready with skills and wisdom as you can be. For surely the fight will come. Ask yourself this question. Am I ready to fight for my life right now? If not, how can I become ever-ready?

Chain Breakers: Be alert and aware of hidden, lurking personal, spiritual, or health dangers. Don't ignore them because they will **never** go away on their own.

Develop a life long strategy. Not just for a month or two, or even a year, I'm talking about a **for-the-rest-of-your-life** strategy.

Mine was 2B4L - To Be For Life™! Everything I considered was in **for-the-rest-of-my-life** terms. After all, I know that I am going to be eating for the rest of my life, so I need to plan appropriately. Are you going to eat tomorrow? The next day and the next? No one thinks about a life long eating plan. You absolutely should if you want to be successful at maintaining a healthy weight.

Realize that food is one of the most powerful, emotionally-charged things in your life. You'll have to interact with food every single day. It's inescapable. You'll make more decisions about food in your life than all other decisions combined. So, you must be ever-ready to meet the challenges and dangers that you will face on your grand weight-loss journey and prevail over them to be victorious. Be sure to enlist the help of others and seek professional help, even if it's short term. Gather your good crew around you and set your sails. Yo Ho! These professionals will help keep your ship on course.

My weight-loss photographs.

At my heaviest, I weighed 282 pounds. This is my official "before" photo I took right after attending my first Weight Watchers meeting. I weighed in at 261 pounds. This was the photo I used as a starting point reference.

Look at our huge distended bellies. Of course I'm talking about me and my dad. (Not my sweet daughter.) Yeah, I easily could have said, "It's all genetics!" But it's not genetics, it was from eating fake, high-fat foods, drinking gallons of soda, and getting no exercise.

This is where you would usually find me, sitting around messing with my computer.

I was always wearing black,
continually trying to fool myself
into thinking I looked slimmer.
It definitely wasn't working.

I had my dad's build for sure,
all "basketball-belly" with skinny
legs and chubby cheeks.
My doctor said this is one of the
most dangerous shapes for men.
It's a prime indicator of heart
disease, diabetes, and
high cholesterol.

Vacations and holidays photos are all I have of the "invisible man." I could only find twelve pictures of myself taken in the last eight years. If it wasn't for these, there would be no photographic evidence that I even existed!

This is a sad statement about how I felt about my own image. Take a look at your own family photo albums. How many pictures do you have of yourself where you are not standing behind something or someone?

I reached my first twenty-five pound goal in February of 2006. It was very exciting! Even better was the six inches I lost from my waist.

Six months into my weight-loss journey,
I was down to 239 pounds.
P.S. Remember the leather jacket!

Here I am at seven months with another
'big" friend. I weighed 231 pounds.
I'd lost another 8 pounds. It was on this
trip to England that I realized I was
completely addicted to cola. I gave up
sodas the week I returned to the States.

Eight months into my journey I reached
225 pound mark. It was about this time
that I absolutely knew that I could do
this for sure.

After six months of losing weight, I knew that I really wanted to see long-term results I needed to join a gym. After staying in the dark TV rooms running on a treadmill for two months, a personal trainer got me out of there and on the weight machines. I started boxing too, and this made a tremendous difference. I went from losing around a pound a week to an average of two pounds weekly.

Still wearing black, but quite a difference from ten months earlier. I'm looking a lot healthier at 214 pounds and seeing some dramatic changes in my body.

Here I am at my goal weight of 200 pounds! The chain at my feet represents the 70 plus pounds I'd lost in just 50 weeks.

Here I am with Karen, my Weight Watchers leader. It's so important to have support along your weight loss journey.

Karen, who recently passed away was a great personal motivator to me. She helped me change my life. There is no greater gift a person can give and I'll forever be grateful to her.

Remember in the earlier photo of me in my tight leather vest size- XXXL? Well here it is now almost wrapping around me. I now wear a large, so I lost three X's!

This is me on the evening I reached lifetime status at
196 pounds. My family was so proud of my accomplishments.
I was proud too. I'm not saying getting there was easy.
But I can tell you it was worth everything I needed to do and
more to become a strong, healthy, visible man again.

I ran my first 10K River Run in 2008 in just 1 hour and 47 minutes. I hit my 500 miles run as I crossed the finish line. You can see I'm making my 2-Legit signs with my hands. I can tell you it was a tremendous moment for me…. a thrilling feeling of victory.

This is the 500 miles run certificate that I received from Nike.com. I've framed it and proudly display it on my office wall. I went on to run over 750 miles that year.

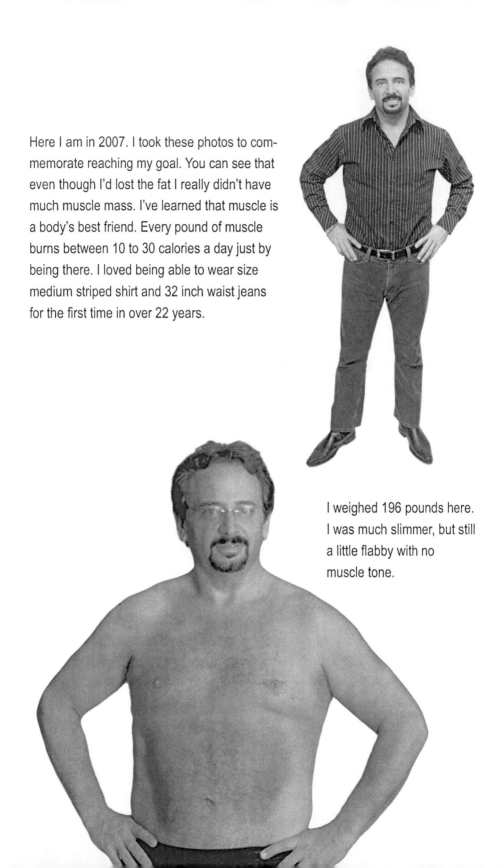

Here I am in 2007. I took these photos to commemorate reaching my goal. You can see that even though I'd lost the fat I really didn't have much muscle mass. I've learned that muscle is a body's best friend. Every pound of muscle burns between 10 to 30 calories a day just by being there. I loved being able to wear size medium striped shirt and 32 inch waist jeans for the first time in over 22 years.

I weighed 196 pounds here. I was much slimmer, but still a little flabby with no muscle tone.

On my four-year anniversary in March of 2010 I'm still wearing stripes. I had to move up to large shirts again, but for a good reason. My chest instead of my belly wouldn't fit into medium sizes any longer. I put on 12 pounds of muscle, which burns 210 calories a week. I think at 49 years old, I actually look thinner, stronger and healthier than I did at 25!

At 201 pounds I've got major muscle tone, a much broader chest, a little ab action, and a gun show too!

Value of the Dolls, 4D

A balanced life
Tai chi helps seniors, 7D

USA TODAY Life
SECTION D

Monday, March 5, 2007

Lifeline

'Rescue Me' crew has eye on new 'probie'

Larenz Tate ('Crash') will guest-star in at least five episodes in the upcoming fourth season of FX's *Rescue Me*. Tate will play a "probie" (probationary firefighter) whom the crew of 62 Truck company is trying to recruit. Tate's appearance on the series will resolve him with his Crash co-stars Jack McGee, who plays Chief Jerry Reilly, and Jennifer Esposito, who will appear as a volunteer firefighter. *Rescue Me* returns in June.

Tate: Will be a firefighter on FX series.

ABC pierces armor of struggling 'Knights'

ABC is yanking *The Knights of Prosperity* from its schedule this week. But the struggling comedy may get a second life with a new white knight: Ray Romano. In last week's episode, he replaced Mick Jagger as the target of *Knights'* hapless burglars. ABC is considering a plan to renew the series for next season, adding new episodes featuring the *Everybody Loves Raymond* star to several already shot with him. Five remain from this season. *Knights' Wednesday* slot will be filled by repeats of *According to Jim* and *George Lopez*.

Comedy fest honors Colbert 'faux real'

Funnyman and faux conservative pundit Stephen Colbert was lauded Saturday as "Person of the Year" by the U.S. Comedy Arts Festival in Aspen, Colo. The star of Comedy Central's *The Colbert Report* said, "What an honor to receive. An honor to receive and an honor for you to give to me." Upon accepting, he also announced plans to write a book. It will be "what is best and worst about America," he said. "You know, it's 20 subjects ... all of the important things, that culture: war, religion, hygiene, sports."

Colbert: Funnyman honored by colleagues.

DVD roundup celebrates The Duke's 100th

Paramount and Warner are teaming up for special John Wayne DVDs timed to hit stores the week of what would have been The Duke's 100th birthday, Due May 22 are special editions of *Rio Bravo* (in $21 and $40 versions.) *The Cowboys* ($26) and the film that earned Wayne a best-actor Oscar, *True Grit* ($20). Wayne, who was born May 26, 1907, died at age 72 from lung and stomach cancer. Also coming soon, six Wayne films making their debuts on DVD: *Allegheny Uprising, Reunion in France, Tycoon, Without Reservations, Trouble Along the Way* and *Big Jim McLain* (each available separately for $13 or in a $50 box set). *True Grit* also will be available in two new Wayne box sets, a $100 14-film Century Collection and a $75 nine-film *Westerns* Collection.

George Michael to christen new Wembley

Singer George Michael will be the first pop artist to play a concert at the new Wembley Stadium, the venue's managing director said Sunday. Michael's gig at the revamped stadium is scheduled for June 9. Three weeks after the venue is to host the Football Association Cup final. "He's no stranger to this great stage, having performed at the old stadium with Wham! at Live Aid and as a solo artist, so this is a fitting first gig in the new stadium," Wembley managing director Alex Horne said in a statement. Wembley's rebuilding was originally due to be completed by Jan. 31, 2006.

By Jen Chaney and Cindy Clark
with staff and wire reports
E-mail lifeline@usatoday.com

USA TODAY Snapshots®

Tips, tools and talk

USA TODAY's Network Journalism initiative has discussion forums, recipes, a Body Mass Index calculator, calorie-burning activities and profiles with photos. Share your stories and advice — with us and with each other.

AFTER

Fighting shape: Tim Taylor takes two boxing classes a week.

BEFORE

Out of shape: Taylor had several medical problems.

Advertising man runs campaign for a new life

Tim Taylor, 46

Hometown: Jacksonville
Occupation: Advertising

Goal: To share his story "to try to give back some of what I've learned and help others. I see heavy people, and I have a place in my heart for them."

Insight for others: "What you believe about yourself — it all comes true. If you believe the best, it will happen."

	Pounds
Height: 5-11	
Weight in August 2005	267
Current weight	183
Loss	84

A sample day

6 a.m.: Beer, drinks a protein smoothie	
7:40 a.m.: Eats a bowl of oatmeal	
8:15 a.m.: Goes to the gym	
9:45 a.m.: Back at office, has protein bar	
12:30 p.m.: Has salad and a cup of fruit	
6:30 p.m.: Dinner	
7:30 p.m.: Snacks on low-fat ice cream bar	
10:30 p.m.: Drinks a protein shake	

Workout	Amount
Runs	3 to 4 miles
Weight train	12 to 20 minutes
Boxing class	2 times a week

What he ate	Amount
Salad	2 cups
Baked chicken	7 ounces
Fresh vegetables	2 cups
	cooked
Wheat bread	2 slices

Heart scare inspires fitness

By Nanci Hellmich
USA TODAY

Tim Taylor, 46, of Jacksonville weighed 267 pounds in the summer of 2005 when he had the biggest health scare of his life.

His heart felt as if it were beating irregularly when he awoke one Saturday morning. He dashed off to see a doctor, who had him rushed to the emergency room. "On the way to the hospital in the speeding ambulance, my heart actually stopped," says Taylor, the owner of an advertising agency. "The [paramedic] said, 'Don't worry. It'll come back.' I think he was trying to be reassuring as I drifted into my next life.

"Terror overtook me at that second," he says. "The accumulation of

Cover story

Please see COVER STORY next page ▶

Please see COVER STORY next page ▶

'Wild Hogs' rumbles to the top with $38 million

Women boost box-office take

By Scott Bowles
USA TODAY

Disney executives knew the timing was right for their John Travolta comedy *Wild Hogs*.

Motorcycling nationwide is on the rise. Free films are competing for older male audiences. And a road-trip film — particularly on Harley-Davidsons with aging stars — seemed the recipe to lure male baby boomers.

What Disney didn't expect was how many women would show up. Hogs, powered by an audience that was 54% female, took in a whopping $38 million, according to Nielsen EDI.

The debut was $10 million more than projections and powered Hogs to the third-highest opening in March, behind *Ice Age* and its sequel.

It also demonstrated Travolta's steadfast appeal to female audiences. Hogs marked the best debut for Travolta and co-star Tim Allen. Travolta's previous mark was 2005's *Be Cool*, which did $23.5 million. Excluding animated films such as *Toy Story*, Allen's previous best was 2002's *The Santa Clause 2*, which did $29 million.

"The women who grew up with (Travolta) since *Grease* have never stopped loving him," says Gitesh Pandya of BoxOfficeGuru.com. "And Oprah raved about the movie. That's two sure-fire ways to get the women out."

Chuck Viane, Disney's head of publicity, also credits the diversity of the cast, which includes Martin Lawrence and William H. Macy.

"They each have their own specific audience," Viane says. "We just didn't expect that they would all show up."

Audiences weren't quite as excited about the other newcomers this weekend, *Zodiac*, the David Fincher film about the serial killer who terrorized Northern California in the late 1960s, met the low end of expectations with $13.1 million, good for second place.

"We think the strong reviews and word of mouth will give us a pretty good run," says Jim Tharp of Paramount, which released the film.

Ghost Rider was third with $11.5 million, followed by *Bridge to Terabithia* with $8.6 million and Jim Carrey's *The Number 23*, which made $7.1 million.

The only other big newcomer, Samuel L. Jackson's sexually charged drama *Smokin' Aces*, did a middling $4 million and eighth place.

Final figures are due today.

In Hogs heaven: Marisa Tomei and William H. Macy

In March 2007, I was selected USA Today's Weight Loss Champion. It was great getting major worldwide recognition for my efforts. All the local TV stations wanted to do features on what I'd accomplished. The local newspaper and radio stations wanted interviews too. I even did radio talk shows here in the States, England, and as far away as Australia. It was really thrilling to be a celebrity for my 15 minutes. The really exciting stuff has been the lives I've been able to touch in a positive way, all the men, women, and children I've had the opportunity to help lose weight!

Every TV station wanted to show action shots of me boxing. I must have thrown 1000 punches that day. It was a lot of fun.

After *SmartMoney* found out that I'd saved over $17,000 dollars simply by losing weight, they featured my story in their magazine. This saving money fact has grabbed more men's attention than just about any weight-loss benefit I speak about. If you tell men how to pocket some cash and get healthy all at the same time, they get interested. You'll be amazed at how much being overweight really costs you a year. You'll be even more enthralled with how much you can save by becoming healthy.

I love being a motivational speaker. It's become a personal passion. Sharing all the lessons I've learned and giving back has become one of the most rewarding aspects of my journey. Helping others to learn how to help themselves and seeing lives changed for the better has helped to give my life real meaning and purpose. I truly appreciate every person my "2" life is allowed to touch. I love sharing 2B4L- "To Be For Life" for a better, healthier, more fulfilled life with anyone who wants to change their own life.

Halfway up the mountain, I fell and twisted my ankle.

Halfway up the mountain, I fell and twisted my ankle. It was at that exact moment when I first saw the wolf out of the corner of my eye: fangs snarling, ears back, and claws dug in, blood-thirsty and headed right for me.

We all remember the nursery story of the three little pigs and the big bad wolf huffing and puffing and blowing their houses down. There are lots of lessons to be learned from this cautionary tale. Don't ignore danger. Don't be a slacker. Don't do anything half-heartedly. Don't do something without a real plan of action. Choose your advisers wisely. When you build anything, choose the best materials and then build it to last. The list of life lessons goes on and on.

Well, halfway up the mountain, I learned another really important lesson about the old wolf as it pertains to weight loss. What, you might ask? Well, just like the three little pigs, it was the realization that the wolf is always at the door.

First allow me to explain, I wasn't climbing an actual mountain when I first noticed "the wolf." I was speaking metaphorically. In reality, I was halfway up my weight-loss mountain when I actually fell on the treadmill and twisted my ankle fairly severely. This started the old wolf huffing and puffing.

My doctor said I couldn't work out for at least two weeks! This was bad news, as running every day had become an important part of my weight-loss routine. Not being able to run brought on feelings of depression. HUFF! Then, because I couldn't workout, my stress level went up. I thought to myself, "Crap! I'll gain back the weight I just lost last week." This started me worrying. PUFF! And how did my former heavy self deal with frustration, depression, stress, and worries? I would EAT! BOOM! The wolf blows your weight-loss house down.

You need to understand that more than 80% of people who lose weight will gain it all back (and usually even more) within two years or less of first losing it. This is the wolf at the door! You must be prepared to outsmart the wolf at every turn to beat these overwhelming odds.

At my current age of 50, I've come to the hard realization that I'm not a young, flexible, quick-healing man anymore. I'll say it, I'm not ashamed or afraid, I'm middle-aged. And, as a forty-five year old man, I thought I knew a few things about life. As it turned out, I really didn't know a lot about anything. The wolf almost got me in my house made of straw.

I had to begin learning again. I began to learn how my body works and how food works within my body. I had to learn how to set personal goals and how to deal with failures and the all-but-certain setbacks. I had to come to the realization that, just because I had lost some major weight, it wasn't ever going to stay off by itself.

I had to start using bricks and mortar to rebuild my life stronger and wiser than before. I had to come to grips with the wolf at my door and, trust me, you'll surely have to learn to deal with him, too.

The wolf's fangs are really the understanding that there are dangers involved in exercising and losing weight. In the last three years of keeping my weight under control, I've twisted my ankle, torn my Achilles tendon, fractured my wrist, and torn a ligament in my lower back. I've had countless colds and flus from touching unclean gym equipment. I've had many more minor aches and pains along the way.

You'll discover that there are other real dangers waiting to get you, like not stretching, improper form when performing an exercise, not giving yourself adequate recovery time, and not getting enough sleep.

Most guys meet their wolf very quickly, as they push themselves much too hard, too quickly, and end up getting hurt. Admit it! It's a macho thing and we've all done it.

You need to recognize that the wolf has razor-sharp claws, too. They are temptations, old habits, and weight-loss plateaus. Other things include not having a solid plan of action, not having an alternative workout plan, getting out of your routine, and not having a solid support system. Not planning today what you're going to eat for every meal and snack tomorrow. Lack of daily motivation and encouragement can blow your house down as well.

You'll need to learn to work from where you are now and progress slowly. When I say slowly, I'm talking about a whole year (maybe two) to reach your main weight-loss goal.

Build your new healthy house on solid ground with the best materials. Get support from your family or friends. Join Weight Watchers or some other weight-loss group or fitness class. Do anything to keep yourself motivated and always learning. Stay far away from any diet pills, they will kill you faster than the wolf ever could.

You must turn the wolf away at **every** opportunity. Do it every single day, at every single meal and at every workout, or he **will** eat you alive!

Chain Breaker: Know that you will have setbacks along the way. Know that, with a solid plan, strong goals, and a never-wavering commitment, you will succeed.

Build a support system and start learning everything you can about living a healthier lifestyle. Have at least two complete work-out gym bags ready every day. Extra shoes, gym clothes, towel etc. always packed and ready. Keep one in your car at all times. It will eliminate the "Oh I forgot something, so I can't work out" wolf.

If you get injured, go to the doctor for help **that day or as soon as possible**. Find an alternative exercise you can do while recovering (example: yoga, swimming, rubber exercise bands or Tai Chi). Doing these things will help keep the wolf from your door and turn your house of straw into a strong brick house.

Commercials on prime-time TV are 11.9 minutes long.

"I don't have any time! Between my work, wife, and the kids, every minute is jammed." You hear this all the time from busy guys our age. Hey, I used to say it all the time myself.

It really does seem like this is true, but believe me, nothing can be further from reality. What if I said I'd pay you $100 for every spare minute you could find in a day? All I'd ask is that you commit to use this new found time for a worthy cause that would change your life for the better. How much time could you find? 5, 10, maybe 30 minutes? Even more?

Where would you look first to find this extra time? Sitting at red lights? Waiting in line at the drive-thru? Would you be surprised to know that, during an average 30-minute prime-time TV show, the commercials takes up 11.9 minutes. The average American watches 3 prime-time TV shows a day. That's at least a whopping 35.7 minutes of commercials every day. That's over 4 hours a week, 16 hours a month, almost 200 hours a year watching commercials that are trying to sell you more fake food and phoney pharmaceuticals.

So if I'd paid you a $100 a minute for this commercial time alone it would total up to $20,000 in a year. Wow! This time would take on a whole new value, a whole new worth to you, wouldn't it? For $20K you would gladly give up your time watching those TV commercials, wouldn't you?

What if I told you that, instead of paying you $20,000, I'd add seven healthy years to your life. That would be worth a lot more than the money, wouldn't it?

Think about it for a moment. Years of time with your loved ones, extra time to really live your life a little more fully. Wouldn't you take the time over the 20K?

Now of course, I can't pay you $100 a minute, and I personally can't add seven years to your life. But I'll share with you how YOU can easily add seven years to your life, for FREE!

I need for you to see that time has a real value and you must spend it very wisely. When I was lying in the back of the ambulance with my heart missing its beat, more time was all I wanted. After lying in the hospital bed thinking that I could drop dead at any moment, believe me, time took on an entirely different and very real value. With my whole being in that I.C.U., I was praying, wishing, gasping with every single breath for just one thing – a little more time. I'm fortunate. By the grace of God, I got more time.

With my weight loss and change of lifestyle, my doctors have told me that I've added at least 7 years (actually closer to 12 years) to my life expectancy. After reviewing my latest test results, my sports medicine physician said: "Absolutely astounding! You are one of the most perfect, fittest, healthiest, specimens of health I've ever encountered in my whole practice of medicine." I can't tell you how much hearing her words of praise meant to me. I'm so proud of what I've been able to accomplish in just 3 short years!

So, how do you add seven years to your life? Just one word, exercise. If you'll do just 11 minutes of exercise three times a day for a total of 33 minutes every day, you can add up to seven years to your life. Not only will you gain more time, you'll help your weight-loss efforts tremendously.

I hadn't exercised at all in more than 19 years, so starting to exercise again at the age of 45 wasn't easy. After my doctors gave me the okay to get started, I began by just jumping up and down 10 minutes a day in my pool. Two months later, I could do a full 30 minutes non-stop.

Then I started walking on a treadmill at level 0 at one mph. After one month, I could do 30 minutes. After two months I was doing 45 minutes at level five at three mph. Today, I easily run three miles at four miles an hour, on an incline of eight, with no problems at all. Some form of exercise is an **absolute must** if you want to lose and keep the weight off. You **can** find the time to exercise if you really value your life.

I want to put a post-hypnotic suggestion into your mind right now. Are you ready? Are you relaxed? Good. As a man, I know you like to have the remote control in your hand any time the television is on. It's a natural thing. Men like to be in control. But from this moment on, every time you touch a remote you are going to think about this one thing...

I have the power to change anything in my life.
Just as easily as changing channels on my TV.
The power to do so is here in my hands.
All I ever need to do is, "Think it, Move it, then Do it."

Now you might not think about this every time you touch that remote, but it's in your mind now for the better. And you will remember that Tim 2 Taylor told you that the power is **"here in my hands"** to change you're life and the lives of those around you for the better.

Every time you sit your big butt in that La-z-Boy and reach for that remote, this thought will be there, reminding you to stop wasting time! Whispering in your ear that time is all any of us really ever have. It's so precious, it's valuable, and it's limited. Please my friend, use it with the experience, knowledge, and sound judgment that I know you possess.

Chain Breaker: Look at your life for wasted time. Especially if it's adding to your waistline. If you're sitting around watching TV or playing video games, reclaim this precious time to actually start living your life instead of watching someone else live his or hers on screen.

Exercise can be cumulative. Start by doing 11 minutes in the morning, 11 minutes at lunch, 11 minutes at night for a total of 33 minutes a day. Start slowly and take it easy. I recommend weight training, aerobic training, and some form of yoga as a good place to begin your exercise program.

Remember to up your exercise time and intensity at least every 28 days, even if it's just a couple of minutes and one level of intensity. In no time at all, you'll be in prime-time shape!

REMEMBER
"here in my hands"

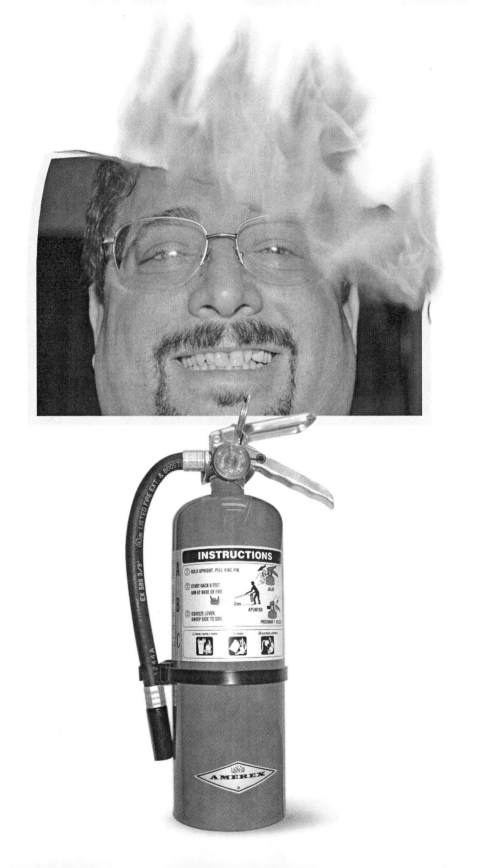

I started a raging fire with my teeth.

The fire was raging out of control, consuming my world. The sad thing was that I'd started the fire myself. I know this sounds crazy, but I started the fire with my teeth! This fire had been smoldering for years, and I didn't even know it. This fire was burning me alive. And this fire had a name – inflammation.

I was dumbfounded when my cardiologist told me that bacteria living around my teeth had caused my gums to become inflamed. This caused my body's fire department (my antibodies) to try to put out this raging fire. The bacteria then blazed a path toward my heart to start inflammation there, too. I discovered that this inflammatory fire could actually kill me. It can cause heart disease or even an actual heart attack. Inflammation is a very real danger for men and women after the age of 40. It can cause myriad health problems. It's vital that you learn what to do the put out these inflammatory fires as quickly as possible.

Your first line of defense is Omega 3. Scientists, nutritionists, and health officials from around the world, and hundreds of medical studies, have proven that Omega 3 (fish oil) can substantially lower inflammation throughout your body. You should be taking an Omega 3 supplement every day. If you can eat wild fish (not farm raised) such as salmon, tuna, or trout, you should absolutely do it. They are all wonderful sources of naturally occurring Omega 3.

Farm-raised fish (and beef) are normally fed on corn, which is high in Omega 6 fatty acids, which can cause more inflammation. So stay clear of them. There are other great oils such as flaxseed and extra virgin olive oil. DHEA (Dehydroepiandrosterone) and CLA

(Conjugated Linoleic Acid) oils are excellent for weight loss, too. All of these essential oils have an amazing health effect on your total body. Beyond reducing Inflammation, these oils help lubricate your joints, help skin to stay young looking, and help your hair to stay shiny (if you still have yours). I believe that taking Omega 3 supplements are absolutely essential to your overall health.

The second line of defense is flossing and brushing your teeth at least twice daily. If you don't do a single thing in this book, do this one easy and effective thing to lower your risk of suffering a heart attack or stroke by an astounding 40 percent, simply by brushing and flossing your teeth! When you're overweight and your self-esteem is low, it's easy to quit caring about your appearance. I hate to admit it, but I had let my dental hygiene go. I never liked my teeth, so I never took very good care of them, I never flossed, brushed on a daily basis, or went to the dentist to get my teeth cleaned.

This combination is like putting old greasy rags on top of dry leaves pouring gasoline on it and then playing with matches. Not very smart. I definitely played with matches by consuming high-fat and bad, cholesterol-laden food and by having lots of stress in my life. I basically torched it up myself! This started the fires raging, first in my teeth, then my joints, arteries, heart valves, and muscles. Even my brain cells were inflamed.

This causes damage such as scarring, hardening, and narrowing of the arteries and major heart disease. When I started losing weight, I decided to start taking better care of myself. I went to the dentist for the first time in years. I chose to get my teeth veneered. This fixed my crooked, gapped, dull, and worn teeth and did wonders for my confidence. I found a new reason to smile and show off my pearly whites. It made me look and feel years younger. But the real benefit was that I had learned to put out the fire of inflammation in my body – and to take better care of myself.

Chain Breaker: HEY, YOU – DON'T IGNORE THIS CHAPTER! YOU WOULDN'T IGNORE A FIRE IN YOUR HOUSE. TAKE ACTION ON THIS TODAY!

Get more Omega 3 in you daily diet, naturally or with supplements, at least 1200 mgs every day. Every other civilized nation recognizes the importance of Omega 3s in your daily diet. They call it an essential to your life supplement. In Italy, if you have a heart attack and the doctor doesn't give you Omega 3, he can be sued for medical malpractice!

Start today brushing and flossing at least twice a day. Go to the dentist and correct or brighten your smile. Then smile more every day.

Getting rid of your Xs permanently!

I hated it. Having to shop In Blg and Tall men's stores. Only being able to choose from 3 colors of dress shirts, blue, white, and tan really sucked. Buying Hawaiian or golf shirts for casual wear, even though I'm not Hawaiian, nor do I play golf. X, XL, XXL, even XXXL. That's a lot of Xs. And all of those "Expand-O-Slacks" that felt like wearing a cinch sack or a garbage bag made me sick. This is the life relegated to those of us who have weight issues. That is, unless you're ready to get rid of your Xs permanently.

I want to help you get rid of your Xs and start shopping at regular stores for L– larges, then M – mediums and, yes, even S – smalls again.

In America, we eat mostly carbohydrates. Currently, our daily diets consist of roughly 51% carbohydrates (non-complex), 34% fats (12% saturated fats), and just 15% proteins. This combination is totally out of balance. It's one of the main culprits that keeps you gaining weight. It kills your ability to lose weight and keeps you hungry all the time, while making you very unhealthy. Let's look at these three branches of foods we eat:

Carbs - carbohydrates (complex and non-complex)

Of the carbohydrates (starches) that Americans consume, most are mass quantities of non-complex carbohydrates. What are non-complex carbohydrates? Basically, they are your convenience or fast foods. Anything highly processed, and made with lots of artificial ingredients and preservatives. They are usually very high in calories, fats, and sodium and low in fiber and nutritional value. It's anything that's been refined, like white flour and white sugar. It's also anything that has to be enriched, any food product which has vitamins and minerals added back into it. Pretty much anything that has never been alive or can't be found in the natural world. These types of carbs turn to glucose very quickly in the body and are a recipe for just two things: being unhealthy and getting fatter!

So what are complex carbohydrates? These are more natural foods, not processed or refined, and lower in sodium and fats. They are naturally high in fiber, vitamins, and minerals. Even though they are sometimes higher in calories, this type of carbohydrate, is good for you. These carbs turn to glucose too, but at a much slower rate. This keeps you feeling fuller longer and keeps your blood sugar at a much more consistent level. By changing from eating so many non-complex carbs to eating more complex carbs, you can greatly enhance your weight loss and vastly improve your overall health.

Examples of complex carbohydrates:

Bran, oatmeal, whole grain pastas, brown rices, potatoes, yams, root vegetables, whole meal and whole grain breads, shredded wheat, beans, peas, and lentils.

Fats

Most men think that all fats are bad, but not all fats are created equal. There are terrible fats, bad fats, and healthy fats. Learning the difference is vital to your health.

The terrible fats are trans fats – hydrogenation creates fatty acids found in fried, fast, and most snacks foods. These fats are deadly to weight loss and your health.

The bad fats are saturated fats – animal products, dairy, eggs, coconut and palm oils used in cooking raise your LDL cholesterol (the bad cholesterol). Try to keep the consumption of these fats to a minimum.

The healthy fats are monounsaturated and polyunsaturated fats – These fats actually lower bad cholesterol and raise your good cholesterol. These are virgin olive oil, fish and flaxseed oils, safflower and sunflower oils, along with most nuts and avocados.

By eliminating the terrible oils, limiting the bad oils, and increasing the amount of healthy oils in your diet, you'll reap major healthy benefits.

Proteins

Proteins are the least understood part of our diets. They should have a more important place in what we eat. Proteins are the body's powerhouse food and are high in antioxidants.

They deliver essential and non-essential amino acids. Increasing your protein intake improves good triglycerides and HDL cholesterol levels. You need to understand that your body doesn't store protein like it does fat. So you have to get your protein daily.

Increasing the amount of protein you eat and lowering your carb intake will force your body to burn more fat for energy. So how much protein is the right amount, and how do you get it?

I've found, and many doctors and nutritionists recommend, that protein should make up 40% of your daily food intake. Before I started on my weight-loss journey, protein made up only 10% to 13% of my diet. That was far below what it should have been. You should be eating at least one gram of protein for every pound you weigh. If you're trying to lose weight or really trying hard to build muscle, I recommend eating at least one-and-a-half to two grams per pound of body weight. Example: If I weighed 250 lbs, I'd need to get 375 grams of protein a day. 210 x 1.5 = 375 grams. That's a whole lot of protein.

How in the world could you eat enough food to get that much protein? Realistically, you can't. If you figure that a seven-ounce serving of chicken contains 49 grams of protein, you would have to eat seven 7oz. servings in a day just to get the proper amount of protein. That's 125 grams per meal if you are eating three meals a day. It's possible, just not very practical.

The best way I've found to get protein is with protein supplements or shakes. I never really wanted to take supplements or drink shakes, but one of my trainers/nutritionists sat me down and spent several hours explaining the real value of getting good-quality protein into my diet. So, I did my own research on the subject and found that what he had told me was true. I started drinking whey protein isolate powder shakes (whey assimilates into the body quickly) with 40 grams per serving. I drink three of these a day. I also drink one Casien protein shake an hour before bedtime (casein assimilates into the body very slowly).

This equals roughly 200 grams of protein from very high-quality sources with a low caloric impact. I get my other proteins from natural foods and vegetables. My suggestion is to start adding protein to your lifestyle slowly. There is no need drink or eat more than 40 grams at any sitting as the body can only use that amount in a given four-hour period. Work toward adding healthy sources of natural proteins into your lifestyle.

Always try for a healthy balance in your eating. Your new eating lifestyle should consist of 50% proteins, 40% complex carbohydrates, and 10% healthy fats. This combination is properly balanced. It keeps you burning fat and losing weight. It helps you build muscle and keeps you feeling full and satisfied longer. You will be truly amazed at how these changes will make you look and feel. Your energy will increase and so will your lean muscle mass. Learning how to make these changes to my lifestyle has helped transform me, and I believe it will help you, too.

I totally got rid of all my Xs! I was wearing medium size shirts and 33 inch waist pants at one point! I've had to go back to wearing large shirts now, not because I gained weight, but because my chest and shoulder muscles have broadened so that I can't keep them contained in a medium anymore. Believe me this is a problem I enjoy having as a 50 year old man!

Protein Bonus:

Protein is essential for building muscle. If you are trying to lose weight and keep it off, then building muscle should be a priority for you. If you really like to eat, you should definitely put on some muscles. Look at body builders, they're eating all the time! Their eating habits seems absolutely crazy, as they eat five to seven full meals every day. Why? Muscles need fuel. Fat burns nothing, but muscles burn carbs and fat 24/7. For the past year, I've been trying to put on 11 pounds of muscle. By adding 11 pounds of muscle, I could burn the same amount of calories as running 2 miles 3 times a week. Just having extra muscle mass actually burns the calories for me. It helps to ensure that I don't gain the weight back, and it looks great. So hit the weights every week and build up those muscles.

Chain Breaker: Curb the carbs, fix the fats, and pump up the proteins. It's easier than you think. Strive for the 50% good proteins, 40% complex carbohydrates, and 10% healthy fats balance with what you eat and drink. I've found this formula to be the essential key to keeping weight from coming back on over time. So many people slowly fall back into their old habits after they have lost weight. By changing to this 50, 40, 10 formula, it will be almost impossible to go back to your old fat ways.

Come on in! The water is fine.

Quick, tell me how much water makes up the human body. Is it 30 percent, 40 percent, or 55 percent? Here's a hint; it makes up over half of our body weight.

Did you guess 55 percent? If you did, you'd have guessed wrong. It's actually closer to 62 percent! It's by far the largest element that makes up our bodies. Your brain is 70 percent water. Your muscles are made up of 75 percent water. 83 percent of what makes up your blood is water. Your lungs are almost all water – a whopping 90 percent.

With bottled water sales at an all-time high, you would think that we Americans would be getting enough water in our daily lives. Realistically, we don't come close.

Would it surprise you to learn that most Americans are two days away from dying from dehydration? On average, we operate at a water deficit of 50 percent, and if you're overweight this deficit can be even greater.

I never drank water. Not a single glass ever. I can remember going years without actually drinking a single glass of water. It was always coffee, tea, or sodas. I know you're saying, "Hey, those have water in them!" This is true. But they're not just water. They contain dozens of chemicals and preservatives and sugars. Did you know that, if you drink eight ounces of cola, it takes four ounces of water just to process the cola through your body? Whereas, if you drink eight ounces of water – well, it processes itself. Our bodies don't have to break anything down to get the water molecules into our blood stream. It uses it just like it comes in.

Think of it like this; would you put maple syrup into your car's gas tank, crankcase, or radiator? How do you think your car would run? It wouldn't. You'd never do this, because you know your car was designed for certain liquids for certain jobs. Gas in the gas tank, oil in the crankcase, and anti-freeze in the radiator. Our bodies are designed to run on one thing – water. **I want you to really understand what I'm saying** – we are constantly putting a chemical syrup in our bodies and expecting it to run fine. It doesn't, it can't, and it never will. **EVER!**

Water is there to help your food digest, burn fat, and build muscle. Water lubricates your joints and lungs. It's absolutely the best fluid to keep your body working properly. Did you know that water is the most powerful solvent in the world? It's so powerful and so good for you!

So, how much water should you drink every day? It really depends on several circumstances. Do you work outdoors in the hot sun all day? Do you work out more than an hour a day? Then you need to drink more water to replace what you are sweating out. If you are taking several vitamins, prescription drugs, or eating a lot of meat and fish, you might also need to increase your water consumption.

A good rule of thumb is three quarts daily. That's 96 ounces or 3/4 of a gallon. If you are really eating around five servings of fruits and vegetables a day, then you're getting about a quart of water from your food. So to get the water you need, you should be drinking eight eight-ounce glasses of water a day.

I don't know about you, but that seemed like a lot of water to me. At least it felt that way when I tried to guzzle that much water down in 3 settings. I couldn't do it. So I went and bought a shot glass, which holds 1.5 oz. and started doing water shots, a few every hour. Six shots equal a little over 8 oz. This helped me feel like I didn't have to be continually drinking down volumes of water. It also helped my body get use to having the right amount of water slowly. Now I love water, I crave it. I always keep two -16 oz. bottles of ice water at the ready. Remember, when you are calculating your water needs, if you drink one cup of coffee or cola (8 oz.) then your body only nets 4 ounces of water.

Chain Breaker: Start slowly trying to drink more water daily. You might feel bloated and need to urinate a little more often. After about five days your body will see that it's getting all the water it needs, and the bloating and frequent urination will go away. Water will help your skin to recover from losing weight. Don't cheat on this, keep it up!

Losing weight saved me $17,021 dollars in one year.

How much do you personally spend on food daily? I mean everything. From that morning mocha latte to that midnight snack. When you start to add it up, it can be very costly.

When I started on my weight-loss journey, I joined Weight Watchers as a support group and as a way to learn more about healthy living. As part of their plan, I had to learn to track the food I ate. Everything you ate had a point value. You needed to write down everything you ate and drank to figure out the points. While I was doing this, I decided to write down what I was spending on what I ate at the same time.

I was surprised to see that, by changing my eating habits for the better, I was changing my spending habits for the better too. I was actually saving money, and not just a little bit. I was saving a lot. I figured out what I spent daily on my unhealthy diet, and I was astounded to see that I was spending about $37 a day (in 2005). That was $259 dollars a week, over $13,468.00 a year on food, just for myself. When you factor in my health care expenses for 2005, this figure came out to $24,628.00!

When I started my weight-loss journey back in 2006, I tracked my food and health care cost for that year also.

My 2006 food and healthcare cost:

• Weight Watchers – $636.00

• Weight loss/nutrition class – $230.00

• Cardiologist (one visit and my last!) – $200.00

• No other doctor visits or drugs this year.

• Vitamins and protein shake mixes – $683.00

• Gym memberships – $540 a year.

• A personal trainer for 3 months, 3 times a week – $450.00

• Personal food cost: daily $12, weekly $84, or $4368.00 for the year.

• Total health care, fitness and food cost – just $6907.00

Add the cost of what I spent on a new, skinnier wardrobe, just for the fun of it – $700.00. My healthier, happier new lifestyle not only helped me lose weight, but it saved me a whopping **$17,021.00**! This amount was so impressive that, when *SmartMoney* magazine heard about what I'd done, they decided to feature my story in a article about how anyone can save money by losing weight.

Let's admit it, as a man, you hate to waste money. At our age, we've learned the value of a buck. We appreciate how difficult it is to keep our hard earned cash in our pockets. For men, only sex trumps the excitement we feel when we make a good deal and save some major cash.

If nothing else in this book inspires you to get off your butt and get moving toward a healthier lifestyle, this chapter should do it. It actually costs less and saves you money to have a healthier lifestyle and lose weight.

Chain Breaker: While you are keeping track of what you eat and drink daily, also record what you spend on food and drink daily. Do this for at least a week so you can get an average daily cost. Then, try to find out what you spent on healthcare last year: Doctor and hospital visits, prescriptions, insurance deductibles, etc. Once you start on your new weight-loss journey, track all of your costs. You might find that your up-front cost for things like Weight Watchers and gym memberships will cost you more. Once you start changing your lifestyle and get healthier, however, that cost will average out. Then watch the savings start rolling in.

She said "I want you to sleep with me tonight."

This is something every red-blooded American man wants to hear from a woman isn't it? "I want you to sleep with me tonight but, with your snoring, it's the sofa for you buddy!" This is something a man hates to hear from a woman.

If you are over the age of 35 and overweight, I can almost guarantee you are a snorer and that you've spent your fair share of time on a sofa or two because of it.

Whether it's a low rumble or a lion's roar, snoring affects your loved ones, your health, and believe it or not, your waistline. Research has shown that men in their early 30s have a 20 percent occurrence of random snoring. By the time they've reached the age of 50, more than 60 percent have a continuous, nightly snoring problem.

Did you know that, if your shirt neck size is 17 or above, those odds jump to 80 percent? Most guys would say, "It's no big deal, so what if I snore?" Let me tell you, brother, you should take your snoring much more seriously.

Medically, it can be an early warning sign of much more serious problems. When I was overweight, I snored like a hibernating bear. My wife hated it. She never got a good night's sleep. My daughter could hear me from her bedroom, with the door closed. I tried all forms of nose drops, nose strips, mouth openers, and jaw holders. Many different types of pills and sprays, even special pillows. Nothing ever worked.

I wasn't getting a good night's sleep either, be it from waking myself up from snoring or from the bruised ribs I got from my wife poking me repeatedly to try to stop me from snoring. I finally went to a doctor who diagnosed me with obstructive sleep apnea. This is where your airways are blocked by relaxed muscles and fat during the night. It only cuts off the oxygen to your lungs, your brain, and your body. It's not really a big deal. Who needs oxygen anyway? I mean, how is going without oxygen for four seconds to four minutes, dozens of times a night, going to affect you?

Let's begin with being tired, having a lack of energy, and bad morning headaches. Then there's the small stuff, like repeatedly sleeping on the sofa or damaging your marriage. There's actually a higher incidence of divorce among heavy snorers. How about having a car accident? There's a higher instance among heavy snorers for this, too. Then there is the big stuff, like high blood pressure, brain damage and heart damage. It also triggers heart attacks and strokes. The morning I had my heart arrhythmia attack, I had awoken from a bad night of snoring.

Snoring and lack of sleep can cause you to gain weight, keep weight on, and make it tougher to lose weight. If you are getting less than seven hours of continuous, good, sound sleep every night, it will have a slowing effect on your metabolic rate. It dramatically cuts the amount of human growth hormone (HGH) that your body produces. This hormone helps build and repair your body nightly, and without it, you are asking for trouble. With lower amounts of HGH, there is a domino effect of higher fat storage and less fat burning. It goes on and on.

Take snoring and lack of sleep very seriously. I no longer have sleep apnea and I no longer snore, either. This is all due to my weight loss. Admittedly, I had to lose 30 lbs. before I really noticed any difference. Once I'd gotten my neck size back to 16-1/2, it all went away. If you want to quit snoring, you've got to lose the weight.

Chain Breaker: Chart how many hours you sleep every night for a week (actual time asleep). If after a week it totals below 45 hours, you need more sleep. Try going to bed at least 30 minutes earlier for 28 days. More sleep means more chance for your body to heal and restore itself, and this will give you more energy during the day. The goal is to get 52 to 56 hours of sleep a week. Get checked for sleep apnea. Focus on reducing your neck size by doing solid cardio work to burn more calories daily. If you smoke or drink excessively, get help to quit and give it up today. Hasn't anyone told you, it's bad for your health – and for your sleep too?

A physicist's theory on being 45.

Einstein was my kind of guy. Maybe not the most macho of men, but he had it where it counts, smarts and an inquisitive zest for the unknown. He was always wondering, "Why?" and was never afraid to challenge the accepted answers. Einstein was a wizard at physics. One of the first things a young Einstein learned about physics is that you can't change it. Gravity is gravity. Time is time. Light is light. It's the same with getting older right? I mean we all get older, get fat, get wrinkles, and we start forgetting things. We go grey or lose our hair and start getting aches and pains. We'll get high blood pressure and have to take handfuls of prescriptions just to stay alive, right? Wrong!

We all get older, that's for sure, but growing old does not mean that you have to surrender to these pre-conceived notions. I'm living proof!

At 45, I had surrendered to all of these preconceived notions. Let me list for you the health problems I was experiencing: I was morbidly obese and had a heart arrhythmia. I suffered from sleep apnea, extreme acid reflux, asthma, and severe allergies. I had a bad back and major joint pain. I was a pre-diabetic and had tingling limbs; I suffered from a low libido, erectile dysfunction, and an enlarged prostrate too. I had extremely high bad cholesterol and very low good cholesterol. I was constantly suffering from colds, flus and sore throats. My stamina and energy levels were almost non-existent.

I laid around all the time sleeping. I was so out of shape I couldn't even walk up one flight of stairs without gasping for air. My mental sharpness had dulled. My memory was starting to have hiccups and gaps. I was taking a dozen prescriptions in an effort to control these ailments.

I believed that this was just a part of getting older. I'd watched these things happen to my dad, so I assumed that it was normal that it was happening to me. It was just part of heading down that old road. I've since learned that these notions are absolutely 100 percent lies! I currently suffer from almost none of my past problems. All of my other physical ailments have vanished without taking prescriptions drugs or diet pills.

Yes, I still have a few allergies a couple of times a year, and this causes my asthma to flare up, but nothing like before. And I do take just one prescription, a testosterone replacement therapy, only because you can't do it naturally, but that is it.

On the whole, all of these so called signs and symptoms of getting old are not affecting me any longer. The human body is so amazing! Once I started giving it what it needed to work properly – natural organic foods in the right portions, fruits and vegetables, water and vitamins, exercise and sleep – everything changed. Just changing these few things made my body actually heal itself.

I feel and look years younger. I've had people guess I was 35! I've had trainers tell me that I've got the heart of a 25-year-old. I can do things I couldn't do when I was 20.

Just like Einstein, I started wondering why I had to have all these health problems just because I was getting older. I quit being afraid to challenge the accepted answers. I, too, developed an inquisitive zest for the unknown. I started learning and changing my life.

Einstein proved Newton's first law, "A body in motion stays in motion unless acted upon by an outside force." I was in motion down that old road and enacted an outside force on my preconceived notions of aging. I changed my direction at the age of 45, and you can, too. While you can't change physics, my proven theory is that you can greatly change how you grow older, for the better.

Chain Breaker: Start fighting your pre-conceived notions about aging today. Write a list of all your ailments and anything associated with aging that is affecting you. Then ask why? What is actually causing these problems? Are you currently taking several over-the-counter or a prescription pills to cope with the problems?

Why not attack the actual cause and heal yourself from the source. I assure you that better nutrition, more exercise, and proper vitamins and minerals will address 90 percent of the physical problems that you associate with aging. Find natural answers and make natural changes. Simply change your programming and change your life!

Did you eat your 6,700 calories today?

How many calories do you consume in an average day? Do you have any idea? Maybe 1,500, 2,500, 3,500 calories? Do you know how many calories you should be eating every day? I didn't have a clue how many calories I should have been consuming, I would just eat exactly like I'd been eating for years. When I started to change my lifestyle, I wanted to see just how many calories I was putting away. So, I started recording what I consumed daily. Every last calorie.

I was dumbstruck by what I discovered. I was eating on average of 6,700 calories per day! For a man my age, I was eating more than three times what I should have been. In fact, I should have been consuming no more than 1,800 to 2,300 calories a day at the most. Instead, I was eating over 46,900 calories every week. That's enough to feed a family of three! I was eating more than my entire day's worth of calories for breakfast alone. I was actually drinking over 1,600 calories every day. Take a look on the next two pages to see what I consumed in calories on any given day. When people talk about mindless eating, that was me. I didn't give a second thought to how many calories were in what I was eating and drinking. Most men don't care or want to count calories or even consider what the actual nutritional value of the so called food they eat is.

Do you know that the average restaurant serves entrees with portions that actually equal three to four servings? When you add an appetizer, salad, bread, or a dessert to that meal, you are eating five to eight times the amount of food you should be consuming at any given sitting. Knowing the correct serving/portion size of a meal is essential to achieving your weight-loss goals. I'll show you what a correct portion is later in the book.

MY ADVERAGE BREAKFAST

INTAKE

1 Can of Coke (right when I got up) = 148
2 Large Fountain Cokes = 400
2 Bacon Egg & Cheese Biscuits = 1120
1 Large Hash Rounds = 460

Total Calories **2128**

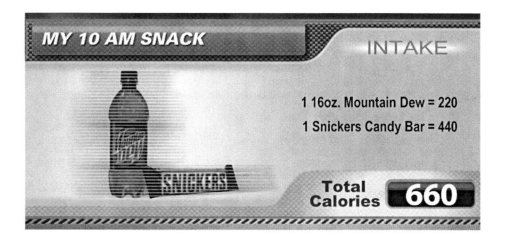

MY 10 AM SNACK

INTAKE

1 16oz. Mountain Dew = 220
1 Snickers Candy Bar = 440

Total Calories **660**

MY ADVERAGE LUNCH

INTAKE

1 Large Fountain Drink = **382** (130mg S)
1 Whopper w Cheese = **1230** (1450mg S)
1 Medium Onion Rings = **309** (491mg S)
1 Large French Fries = **478** (816mg S)
1 Piece of Apple Pie = **320** (290 mgS)

Total Calories **2719**   **Total Sodium** **3177**

MY 3 PM SNACK

1 12oz. Coke = 148

1 Bag of Potato Chips = 300

Total Calories **448**

MY ADVERAGE DINNER

Texas Tonion = **1130** *(2320 mg S)*
Blue Cheese Dippin sauce = **100** *(310 mg S)*
Divided appetizer by a third = **410** *(876 mg S)*
Long horns Flo's Filet 9oz = **550** *(630 mg S)*
Caesar Salaid Dressing = 2 oz **280** *(430 mg S)*
Caesar Salad cheese /crutons = **80** *(N/A mg S)*
Baked Potato with butter **360** *(95 mg S)*
Key lime pie = **630** *(270 mg S)*
3 tsp of Steak sauce = **45** *(840 mg S)*
5 pieces of bread = **500** *(N/A mg S)*
3 sweet teas =**135** *(N/A mg S)*

Total Calories **4220** **Total Sodium** **5771**

MY DAILY CALORIC INTAKE

Total Number of Calories Eaten - 10175

Total Milligrams of Sodium - 8949

Most Americans dine out at an average of seven neighborhood restaurants. Think about it; you don't eat Indian cuisine, then Korean, then Mexican all in the same day. We usually eat the same meals at the same seven restaurants over and over. It may vary some, but mostly it's the same places and the same meals. That's why we call what we eat our favorites.

If you discover that the portion of food served at your favorite restaurant is too large (and I guarantee you it is), start your meals with a Pre-Overs™ bag. Instead of getting a left-overs bag when the meal is done, ask your waitress to bring you a take home container before your meal arrives at the table. Start by cutting your food in half and take it home for lunch the next day. I keep a cooler with ice blocks in my trunk that I store my pre-overs in to keep them fresh until I can get them to a fridge. I also keep my snacks, fruit, and a protein shake in there, too. Over the next month, start cutting your meals into thirds instead of halving them. This way, you still get to enjoy some of your favorite meals but at a third of the calories. Plus, you can have a leftover third and a third to share with a family member. You'll get closer to a proper portion size, lose weight, and save a lot of money.

If you drink a lot of coffee, soft drinks, wine, or beer, I guarantee you are drinking a ton of empty calories every day. When I say a lot, I mean more than two 8 oz serving a day. Did you know that the FDA recommends that you consume no more than one 8 oz serving of soda in any given day, and that it should be considered "a treat." I've already shared the dangers of soft drinks, but other drinks sweetened with refined sugars or HFCS and artifical sweeteners can really be bad for you too. Beer and wine are often very high in calories and very low in nutritional value also.

You should start drinking more water, green or black teas, and fresh organic fruit or vegetable juices. All of these contain no or low calories per serving. They are high in antioxidants and nutritional value and will help you lose weight long term.

Chain Breaker: Find out how many calories you are eating daily. Cut back to under 2,000 a day. Pick your favorite seven restaurants, then pick a low calorie dish of 500 to 600 calories total from each restaurant. Then at your favorite restaurant, you can order with confidence while controlling your portions size. If you can't do this, cut the serving into thirds take home the 2/3 pre-overs. Split the meal with a friend or two, or your wife and save some money! Dump the sodas, start drinking 6 to 8 glasses of water, green and black teas, fresh fruit or vegetables juices everyday. These strategies really do work.

Vitamins, minerals, pills, and potions.

People want simple reasons and quick answers. The two questions I get asked the most concerning my weight loss are "Did you get a divorce and a new girlfriend?" And "What pill did you take to help you lose all that weight?"

Isn't that funny? I find it fascinating. I think I can understand the first question, being a man of my age. Most people figure that some major life change such as a divorce or getting a new, hot babe for a girlfriend would be a significant enough reason to dramatically change my life. Let me assure you (and my wife) that this wasn't the case.

As far as the second question, let me assure you that there is not a pill you can take to really lose weight either. There's a billion-dollar industry built around the illusion that there are pills, powders, and potions to help you lose all the weight you want easily, without changing what you eat or having to exercise. It's all HOGWASH!

Sure, there are tons of things that can make you lose weight, but once you stop taking the pill or powder or potion, the weight will most definitely come right back. And trust me, the side effects or consequences of using these so-called miracle weight-loss products will follow you long after the manufacturer is sitting on a beach in the Caribbean spending your money without a care for your health or well-being. However, there is a healthy and safe way to use the right pills and powders to help you lose weight.

A year after I started my weight-loss journey, I had my doctor perform a special test called a Spectra Cell test. It's expensive (around $800 bucks), so make sure your insurance covers it before you ask your doctor to do it for you. It measures all the vitamins, minerals (micro nutrients), and hormone levels in your body.

When my results came back, I was shocked to discover I had massive vitamin and minerial deficiencies. My doctor showed me that, if I would simply give my body the vitamins and minerals it needs, it could right itself and start functioning correctly, given enough time. So, instead of believing in some magic pill pushed on me by a big pharmaceutical company, or some back room mixer of potions, I decided to try to follow a natural path back to health and vitality.

Believe it or not, it was the first time anyone, especially a doctor, showed me that, because we have so long deprived our bodies of the actual things it needs and requires to function, it's practically impossible for it to do what it's supposed to do. Once I saw that I was deficient in so many areas, I knew my doctor was right. This began my supplement safari.

So, what are vitamins anyway? They are organic compounds essential for human growth and nutrition. Our body requires them in small daily quantities, because they cannot be made by our body or they're difficult to get through a normal modern diet.

What are minerals? They are inorganic substances needed by our body to continue in good health, things like potassium, calcium, sodium, magnesium, and zinc. I discovered that vitamins and minerals have many different doses and different absorption rates. Some should be taken at different times of the day or night some with meals and others on an empty stomach. It's a real science unto itself. But once you get it worked out, it is very easy to get into a simple routine of taking daily supplements. My results have been nothing short of astounding!

I had the test re-done one year later and the results were absolutely perfect! Every single vitamin and mineral was in the perfect to excellent range. My doctor said that she's performed hundreds of these tests over the past three years, and she has never had a single patient 100 percent in the perfect range ever before. How's that for a major comeback?

Even the lab personnel where impressed. Was accomplishing this easy? Yes and no. It takes a serious commitment to not just lose weight but, more importantly, to become a healthy person again.

Of course, there are many natural and health-affirming vitamin and minerial supplements you can take to greatly improve your overall health and body functions. I've included a list of the supplements, vitamins and minerals I take daily on page 126.

98

But don't just take what I take. You have to take what you need specifically for your body's deficiencies. Of course there are generalities, like a good multi-vitamin (split it in two – take half in the morning and half in the evening), C, D, and the B vitamins.

You also need to understand that there are fat-soluble vitamins and water-soluble vitamins. Fat-soluble vitamins needs to be eaten with food (healthy fats) to be broken down and absorbed properly. Water-soluble vitamins break down in water to be absorbed properly. Get with your doctor and a nutritionist to put together the best solution to meet your body's needs.

So, why are these vitamins and minerals so important to weight loss? If you give your body what it needs nutritionally, it doesn't need to hold onto fat to keep it just functioning. It become more efficient at burning calories, eliminating waste, and a whole host of other vital things that extend your life and make you a much healthier person. **Chain Breaker:** Like I always say, "You don't know until you go!" So, go to your doctor. Take this book with you and tell them what YOU want to do to save YOUR OWN life.

Get a Spectra Cell test done if you can afford it and then identify any deficiencies. Make sure the doctor checks to see if there are any adverse reactions or side effects that may arise from any supplement you take with any medications you currently may be taking.

After getting their dosage recommendations, start taking your natural supplements daily. Do NOT start taking 20 supplements on day one. Start very slowly and add a new supplement every few days. This gives your body a chance to get used to these new supplements and allows you to better judge any interactions. Be sure to give a list of any medications you are taking or that have been prescribed from any other doctor you may be seeing. That way, they can review and advise you of any strange side effects or dangers involved with taking any supplements.

Don't be freaked out by the color or the smell of your pee! Your body will use what it can and then urinate the remains out. It will return to a normal color and smell in a few weeks, as your body gets better at breaking down the vitamins and minerals.

Understand that it takes awhile for your body to adjust to having every-thing it needs to thrive, but in time you too will be amazed at the difference it will make with your weight loss and long-term health management.

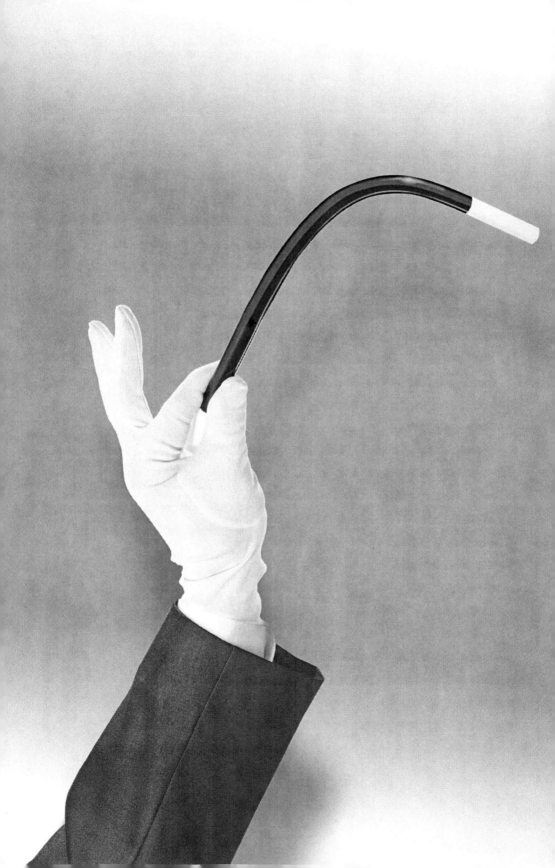

What was supposed to be hard was soft.

Okay you know I had to address this subject, as uncomfortable as it is for most men our age, so let's go there. It's one of the most asked question I get from men when they have a chance to talk in confidence.

Did losing all that weight help your penis work better? You know, bring it back to life? Get it out on the launching pad? Put some magic back into the ol' wand again? Euphemisms aside, dealing with what was once hard and now is soft is a very delicate issue for most men. Men don't want to think about it, much less even talk about it. Most men wouldn't even talk to their doctors about it until the debut of the "little blue pill" several years ago. But erectile disfunction (ED) is a very real problem for overweight men over the age of 40. Heck, it's a real problem no matter how old you are.

So, here's the hard (or soft) question; did I suffer from ED when I was overweight? And did losing weight and getting healthier improve the problem? The answer to both questions is yes.

I'll admit it, when I was overweight, along with losing my youthful vibrant personality, I lost my ability to maintain an erection. Oh, I could get the rocket to the launching pad, it was after the launch that, "Houston, we have a problem!" Maintaining an erection was my problem. For some men, the inability to get an erection at all is the problem.

Suffering with ED is one of the most crushing blows to a man's ego and self-esteem. It cuts to the core of our masculinity, as if being fat and not feeling attractive to the opposite sex wasn't bad enough, you experience ED on top of it all. Life can suck sometimes. It's all very disheartening. It truly was for me.

You might be surprised to learn that 50 percent of all men over the age of 40 experience some form of ED. It also shouldn't surprise you that 50 percent of the male population in America over 40 are considered overweight. Strange coincidence? I think not.

I truly believe that there is a direct correlation between being overweight and experiencing some form of ED. Don't get me wrong, there are many other possible causes for ED: high blood pressure, diabetes, high cholesterol, low testosterone levels, stress, smoking, drinking alcohol, drug abuse, and the very medicines used to treat all of the above mentioned ailments.

WAIT A DAMNED COTTON PICKIN' MINUTE HERE! All of the above mentioned ailments are actually caused by just two things – being overweight and doing unhealthy things to your body. High blood pressure, diabetes, high cholesterol, low testosterone levels, and stress are often directly associated with or caused by being overweight. So basically, the main of reason men over 40 experience ED is because they are overweight!

You won't hear this truism heralded by any of the giant pharmaceutical companies in their ads for ED treatments. They know that if men really wanted to solve the real problem of being overweight, they wouldn't need the temporary fix for their ED problems. Yeah, they might have a paragraph buried in their website somewhere that says "Loss of weight, exercise, and quitting smoking may help with ED," but they want you to buy their products. It's their business.

Wake up guys! Almost all of your current health problems can be directly linked to being overweight. I can tell you that virtually all of my health problems were caused by being overweight.

As for smoking, drinking alcohol, and drug abuse, – let's get real here for a minute. If you are addicted to these unhealthy habits, getting and keeping an erection is the least of your problems. If you suffer from any of these addictions that are really used to cover up pain in your life, you must seek professional help and address them first, then worry about your penis later. It's common sense, man!

Now that you know the real reason you are experiencing ED is because of your weight, let's do something to solve it. I can wholeheartedly assure you that losing weight can restore and even enhance your ability to achieve and maintain an erection, and improve your sexual endurance to boot.

It can even add up to an inch to your penis length. How's that for a convincing reason to lose weight? (Don't let your wife read this last statement, or she'll have you on a treadmill running like a dog tomorrow, buddy!)

You need to understand that, most of the time, ED is related to circulation problems. It can be a sign of major cardiovascular disease, so you should definitely speak to your doctor about any erectile dysfunction you are experiencing. What I want you to understand is how being overweight affects your penis and its ability to go from the hanger to the launch pad and then into orbit.

If you haven't exercised, undoubtedly you'll have a lowered lung capacity. This means that you're getting less oxygen in your blood and have slower overall circulation. Then there is the fact that, for every pound of fat you have on your body, it takes about a mile of blood vessels to support those fat cells. If you're 50 pounds overweight, that's 50 miles of extra blood vessels in your body. This causes your weak heart to have to work even harder to pump your poorly oxygenated blood on an extra 100-mile round-trip journey just to keep you alive. This can cause higher blood pressure. Your body has to make a choice, keep your penis erect or keep you alive. It chooses to keep you alive.

Understand that the blood vessels and tissues in your penis are very fine, and the blood flow control valve is sensitive to levels of nitric oxide (or NO), which is a gas carried by the blood to the penis. Low circulation means lower blood flow to the penis, and less nitric oxide in the penis means fewer strong or no erections altogether.

If you are overweight and have many of the problems associated with being heavy, such as low testosterone, this can be a major cause of ED also.

Now for the good news; Once I started losing weight, I began to notice that the size of my penis seemed to get larger in both directions. Once I'd started exercising, especially running, I noticed that I began to have serious morning erections again. This led to sustained erections anytime I wanted one. I feel like a 19-year-old again. As my gut and that pooch of fat over my pelvis began to disappear after losing around 50 pounds, I noticed that my penis really seemed longer. Okay, I measured it, and it actually was over an inch longer than the last time I measured it. (Come on admit it, at 17 we all measured it.)

Scientists say that reducing the fat around the pelvic region allows for deeper penetration during intercourse, thus giving your partner the sensation of a longer penis and visually creating the appearance of a longer penis. Whatever, science dudes!

I don't care what you want to say, all I know is that my erectile disfunction has virtually disappeared, and what was once soft can now get and stay hard again.

Mornings are flag-raising events again. My masculinity and self-esteem have been restored where it counts. The magic is back! All from losing weight, exercising, and living a healthier lifestyle.

I'm not promising anyone that just losing weight will help or even cure any ED you might be experiencing. And if you want or need help achieving a satisfying sexual experience, brother, by all means go for it! There is no shame whatsoever in seeking help. I'm an advocate of getting help for sure. Who am I to say that a pill or any other means of having a great sex life isn't your prerogative? I just wanted you to know that there are other possibilities to look into and to offer you another really great incentive to lose your excess weight.

Chain Breaker: First, if you are experiencing any form of ED, go see a doctor. Don't just ask for a pill right off the bat. Make him or her understand that you want to try a natural way to improve your ED while seeking a treatment for it. Let them know you are going to lose your excess weight and get back in shape.

Get tested for cardiovascular disease, low testosterone levels, and high estrogen levels (which is common if you have metabolic syndrome). Know that if you are in chronic pain, prolonged use of pain medication can be a major cause of ED too. Ask your doctor for a different pain management alternative.

Secondly, get the okay to start exercising. Then start exercising at least three times a week, 30 to 45 minutes per session. Particularly try to start doing aerobic exercise as it's a very effective way to help remedy erectile dysfunction. And it's cost effective, too. There is no $6 to $10 dollars per erection cost associated with doing aerobic exercise. Aerobic exercise increases your overall lung capacity and circulation, lowers stress, and naturally raises testosterone levels. It will improve your stamina and help you burn fat more effectively. Lastly, your partner will greatly appreciate the positive effects your weight loss will have on your sex life together.

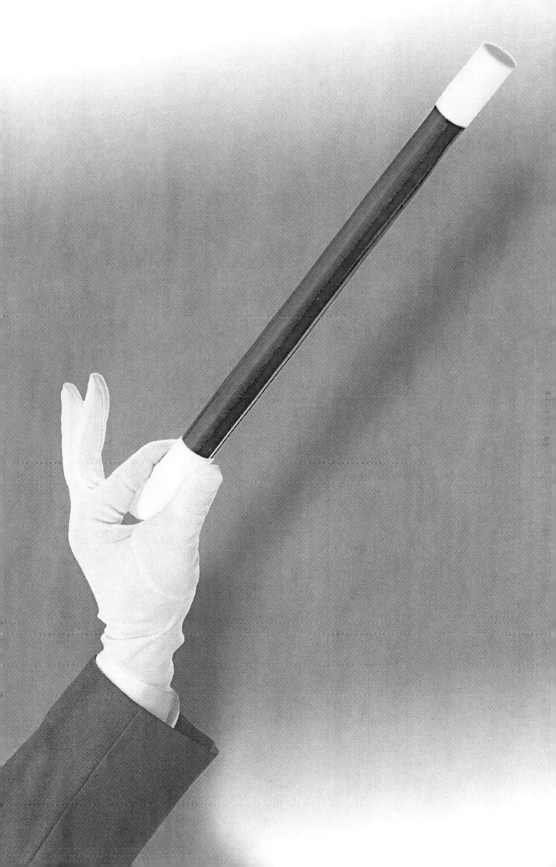

Tennis balls, softballs, and a football.

You know I had to follow up a chapter on ED with a chapter on BALLS! I know you are asking yourself, "What could a chapter on tennis balls, softballs, and a football have to do with helping me lose weight?" Well, I'm going to tell you right now.

You are eating too much food. Way too much food for your own good. The average person in America consumes around 1,800 pounds of food a year. That's almost five pounds of food every friggin' day! Dude, and you wonder why you're getting fatter?

Understand that this average was compiled way back in 2002 by the US Department of Agriculture. Now we all know and trust how accurate our government studies are, right? Yeah, right!

Through my personal experience with, and through input from other overweight men over the age of 35, I've found that the actual amount of food consumed, especially if you eat out at least one meal a day is closer to 6.2 pounds every day. That's 2,263 pounds of food a year.

THAT IS MORE THAN A TON OF FOOD A YEAR! And this does not count the average of 48 gallons of sodas you drink to wash all that food down with.
More than a ton. Just sit with this thought for a minute. Let this fact sink in... **A TON.**

This chapter is about learning how much food is actually enough. It's vital that you gain a good understanding of the size and volume of food you should eat daily.
To help you learn this, you've got to have some balls. Let's start with the football.

While on a business trip, I had an opportunity to see the exhibit Bodies Human.

For those of you who don't know, this exhibition features a plastination or the freezing of actual complete, real human bodies without skin. It's really an astounding and informative exhibit, albeit a little morbid and disconcerting at times.

As I was in the early stages of losing my weight, I was very interested in the deposits of fat in different places within the body. One thing intrigued me beyond all the other amazing sights. It was the size of these peoples stomachs.

All of their stomachs were about the size of a pack and a half of normal playing cards. It's actually very tiny, much smaller than I'd imagined. I had always thought that our stomachs were much larger. I started doing research on stomach size.

Did you know that the stomach is the single most expandable organ in the human body? It can expand to over seven times its normal size. How big is that? About the size of a regulation NFL football. Now if you're overweight and eating 6.2 pounds of food every day, guess how big your stomach constantly stays? You guessed it! The size of an NFL football! And you wonder why you're hungry all the time? (Take a look at the pictures on page 113 and 114 for an actual size comparison.)

The only nonsurgical way to reduce the size of your stomach is to eat less food consistently and do so for a long amount of time (about six months to a year).

It's simple physics, fewer pounds in, less stretch, and less stretch equals a more full feeling with less food. Understand that one big Thanksgiving or other holiday meal can wreck 6 months of reduction. So, be careful; once you decide to consistently eat less daily poundage, you've got to stick with it to be successful.

So, how do you know how much to eat at any given meal? Tennis anyone? Tennis balls - three to be exact. Three tennis balls worth of food in volume should be the proper amount of food you should be eating at any given sitting, breakfast, lunch, and dinner, and even less with snacks.

I know that this is a major shock to almost all of you. I can hear the majority of you saying, "Three tennis balls? Man, I eat that much in three bites. I'd be starving all the time!" Believe me, I hear you, but this is where proper nutrition, timing, and eating filling foods come into play. You need to get rid of your fatty, high-carb, low-nutrition foods.

Then begin eating all natural, healthier, complex carbs, more proteins, more water- and fiber-filled foods. You'll feel fuller longer and reduce your blood sugar spikes too. This will, in turn, lower the negative chemical reactions and hunger signals in your stomach and digestive tract, and soon your metabolism will speed up.

You need to understand that scientists have proven that our bodies on a subconscious level force us to try and eat the same weight of food every day. Your body "remembers" or measures how much actual weight in food you take in daily. It complains (grumbles) and sends hunger signals to the brain if you haven't eaten the same weight of food each day.

In essence, if you ate 6.2 pounds of food yesterday, then your body tells your mind that it wants and needs 6.2 pounds of food today. It doesn't care how nutritional or healthy the food you consume is, it just wants the same volume in weight every day.

This is where the distorted super-sized portions come into play. We've all been tricked by the fast food giants, major restaurant chains and, yes, even our own mothers into thinking that more is better and a better value. You couldn't be more wrong!

More isn't always better, especially when it comes to food. Remember earlier in the book when I told you how the major restaurant-chain portions were made up of 3 to 5 servings in just one meal? Well let's take a closer look at what the average American male consumes from the time he sits down at a restaurant to the time he pays the bill.

Think about your last dinner out at a steak restaurant. You sat down, and they brought you bread, then you ordered that big onion ring appetizer thing. Then you ordered that 12-ounce steak, big baked potato, and oh yeah, it comes with a salad. Oh and could we get some more bread when our meal comes out? And you clean your plate like Mom told you to do. Then my favorite question from the waitress, "Did you leave room for dessert?" Sure! That piece of pie sounds good, but your wife wants cake. We can get both and share. Does this sound familiar? You know it does.

Would you be surprised to know that the meal that we just described is over five times the proper servings. Let's break it down.

• Bread - two slices of bread (1.44 ounces) is a proper serving.

The amount of bread an average man eats at a dinner out is six servings!

• The fried onion appetizer - just seven stalks would be a serving.

Twenty stalks are what is consumed on average – three times a proper serving.

• The salad - it's two times a proper serving size in volume, four times a proper serving of salad dressing.

An average full steak dinner served
at an American restaurant is equal to
four and a half softballs in volume.

Imagine swallowing four and
a half softballs just for dinner!
That's absolutely crazy!

Then the main course:

- That 12-ounce steak is almost two times the correct serving size. 7 ounces is the correct portion.
- The big baked potato is usually two times the proper serving and what you put on it, the butter and sour cream, is usually two times a proper serving.
- The dessert is usually four times the proper serving!

There is also a whole day's worth of sodium and fat, both three times the amount you should consume in any given meal. I know most people don't eat like this at every dinner, but even if you eat like this only on Saturday night, it's equivalent to eating five extra dinners a week! I could talk about all the calories involved in this meal, and your eyes would glaze over and you'd put the book down and never pick it up again. Men just don't want to count calories. Of course you know the calories in this meal are completely insane and totally out of control, but it hasn't stopped you from eating! What you need is a fresh and different way to actually see the problem.

Guys are visual, so allow me to help you visualize this problem. I want to put this into terms any man can grasp. (Here is where the softballs come in.) Imagine swallowing four and a half softballs just for dinner! This is exactly what you are doing. This steak dinner is equal to four and a half softballs in volume; it's absolutely crazy!

The average dinner served in American restaurants are at least four softballs in volume. The fact that we actually eat this much is really unbelievable. I mean, what are we thinking? That's just it... we are not really thinking at all. We just unconsciously eat whatever is served to us. My friend, you've got to wake up! You've got to start thinking for yourself about what kind of foods you're eating and how much food you're putting into your body daily. Our understanding of how much food is proper and healthy to consume is so off base, so out in left field, that it's hard to comprehend. Four and a half softballs are a long way from three tennis balls in volume.

This is why you have to grow a pair, man up, and get determined to shrink your stomach size back to normal. Start learning about the right types of food and drinks to consume. But most importantly get your serving and portion sizes under control and keep them that way **for the rest of your life!**

If you want to lose weight and really keep it off long term, learning, changing and applying this knowledge about portions is absolutely essential to your success.

Chain Breaker: The right amount of food to consume at any sitting should be no more than three tennis balls in volume. This includes appetizer, bread, salad, the main course, and dessert combined. Three tennis balls total. Think about what you ate last night. I bet it was way more than three tennis balls in volume. I suggest that you actually buy a tennis ball and carry it with you for a week. Hold it next to what you're eating at every meal and see if you are eating the correct volume. By consuming much smaller meals, and improving the overall nutritional value of each meal, it will positively make a huge difference in your weight loss.

Personally, I hate counting calories. But you might like to try it for at least a little while. I suggest you try looking up some of your favorite meals and actually **know** how many calories you are really consuming. There are dozens of calorie counters online and, yes, there's an app (hundreds of them) for that too. They are super helpful and will be an eye-opening experience for you, even if you do it for one day. You will be shocked.

The USDA recommends, as a rule of thumb, that a sedentary male who is 5'11" and over the age of 30 should consume no more than 2,000 calories a day. So if you eat only three meals a day, that's only 666 (an ominous number) calories per meal.

If you add up just condiments you use daily like ketchup (1 tsp is 60 calories), mayonnaise (1 tsp is 100 calories), dressings (1 tsp. is 120 calories), BBQ sauces (1 tsp. is 30 calories) or butter (1 pat is 20 calories), a packet of sugar is 15 calories and 1 of those little things of non-dairy creamer is 10 calories. Just adding in all these additional calories you can easily average an extra 580 calories a day. So remember to count condiments too.

Remember to add in whatever you are drinking also. Every regular can of soda adds at least 143 calories; one bottle of beer is usually 145 calories; one regular glass of wine is 127 calories. Drinking just 3 drinks a day (most people drink 6 to 8 a day) easily adds up to at least 430 calories. If you combine the calories from just drinks and condiments, it can total well over 1010 calories of stuff with almost no real nutritional value at all. Deduct these calories from a 2,000-calorie-a-day food plan, and you're left with only 990 calories for real food! Do you think you could eat just 330 calories per meal? I double-dog-dare you to try. Can you see how distorted our eating habits have become?

It's time to begin keeping your eye on the ball. Size up what you're eating, size down your portions, and then stay with it for the rest of your life. You'll start losing weight and keeping it off forever.

The stomach is the single most expandable organ in the body. It can expand to over seven times its normal size. How big is that? About the size of a NFL football.

The average human stomach (empty) is about the size of a pack and a half of normal playing cards. Much smaller than you might think.

THE ORIGINAL
BED BUDDY™
[MICR]OWAVE HEAT-PACK

[...]T HEAT FOR ACHES & PAINS
[F]ROM YOUR MICROWAVE
IN 2 MINUTES !

MADE IN THE USA

Non-Toxic & Reusable
a TCP Reliable Company
USA / CANADIAN PATENTS
MADE IN CANADA BY CRYOPAK INDUSTRIES (2007) ULC

cryopak
PROTECTICE

cryopak
a TCP Reliable Company
www.cryopak.com
VANCOUVER 1-800-667-9573
MONTREAL 1-888-423-7253

PAIN RELIEF
[...]E IT
[...]PY ROLL-ON
[...]LATED VANISHING SCENT
[...]AMIN E

Walgreens
COLD
PACK

CAUTION: READ DIRECTIONS BEFORE USE
DIRECTIONS FOR COLD PACK USE:
• Place this gel insert in the freezer for at
least 2 hours before using.
• Remove from the freezer and place gel
insert inside the white protective [...]
NOTE:
• Never apply this frozen gel [...]
[...] skin without first p[...]

[...] the protective wrap.
• Apply to affected area for no more th[...]
30 minutes at one time.
• After treatment, remove this gel inser[...]
from the protective wrap and return [...]
the freezer, allowing at least 2 hours
between treatments.
WARNINGS
• USE ONLY AS DIRECTED. Always use [...]
gel insert with the protective wrap.
Direct application of this gel insert to t[...]
skin could cause frostbite.
[...] the [...]ed COLD PACK is uncomfo[...]
[...] cold and pain, discontinue using [...]
[...]prod[...] immediately.
COLD [...] should not be used by [...]
[...]sensitive to [...]

THE V[...]
C[...]
B[...]

IMPORTANT:
Reseal after opening

FLECTOR® PATCH
NDC 60793-411-05
(diclofenac epolamine topical p[...]
1.3%

[...]M EACH)

Are you tired, sore and achy? I've got the tricks that will fix!

If you've read this far in the book, you know that exercising is an absolute must in losing weight and keeping it off. Let's face it guys, we ain't spring chickens any more.

Even when you were young and played that weekend flag football game with your buddies, come Monday morning you were paying the price. PAIN and SORENESS!

Every dang muscle ached, even sitting hurt, and you felt exhausted. Why do you think you and your buddies quit playing those weekend games? You got too old and out of shape to do it anymore, and you hated the aches and pains afterwards.

I'm not going to sit here and lie to you. If you start exercising, you are going to have some aches and pains. The good news is that you don't have to hurt so badly, or for very long either, if you learn a few tricks about pain and inflammation management.

First, some physiology stuff. When you exercise muscles, they are actually tearing. These tears release a substance called lactic acid. This is the "burn" you feel when you're pumping iron or running really fast. Lactic acid causes inflammation, and inflammation causes pain. The other type of soreness or pain you're feeling is from slight sprains, achy joints, and overly tight muscles. This is caused by not warming up and stretching properly before exercising or not performing your cool-down stretches after your workout.

These are the two main reasons for the soreness you experience the next day.

It's essential to control soreness and help counter inflammation by learning to stretch correctly. This is very important when you begin a new exercise program. Injury, pain, and soreness rank as the top reasons why men over the age of 35 give up exercising. Nothing I've found in my four years of losing weight and maintaining it is a greater cause of failure than pain. If you are going to be successful, it's essential that you learn several pain avoidance techniques and proper pain management.

Pain avoidance

You've heard it said that, "A good offense is the best defense!" Nowhere is this more true than when starting an exercise routine. You must go on the offense with a strategic plan of action before you encounter injury, pain, and soreness. Beginning with personal equipment, and the most important item is your shoes.

Shoes are the foundation on which almost all exercise is performed. I see guys wearing their beat-up, 3-year-old tennis shoes to the gym. Then I listen to them complain about back pain, leg pain, shin splints, and not surprisingly, foot pain. Fortunately, I had a trainer who spotted my error early on in my weight-loss journey. He showed me that having the right shoes counters ankle and foot injury. It also softens knee and hip joint impact and overall shock to your body. It also helps keep your spine and posture correct while exercising.

He advised me to buy a new pair of shoes after losing every 25 pounds. This is because, as your weight shifts, so does the wear pattern of the shoe. I know this seems extravagant, after all the shoe still looks good from the outside, but it's what's on the inside that matters.

Look at the heels of your old shoes. Are they worn on the left or right edges? Look at the ball of the foot. Is it worn also? Look on the inside. Can you see the pattern of your toes imprinted into the insoles? If so, it's new shoe time.

I strongly suggest that you find a running specialty store. They usually have experienced runners as salespeople, who truly understand sizes, foot roll, arch support, shoe weight, and impact zones. Share with them that you're going to start a walking or running program on asphalt, off-road, or on a treadmill. They can get you in the proper shoe for your current weight and for what you're trying to accomplish. Also, as you lose weight and need to replace your shoes, you can bring in your old pair and they can actually evaluate your wear pattern and possibly recommend a better shoe for you.

The right shoes are your first and best offensive measure against injury, pain, and soreness.

The next best offensive move is stretching. So many men just start exercising and, right off the bat, they wind up injured. Stretching and warming up your muscles slowly for at least 10 minutes before you start any type of exercise is important. It's even more important if you exercise in the morning. In fact it can actually save your life.

Most people don't know this, but while you sleep your blood vessels and veins constrict dramatically. This means blood flow to your muscles is restricted, especially to an important muscle, your heart. Your blood thickens and gets very sticky during the night, especially if you're overweight. This thick and sticky, slow-moving blood can increase your chances of getting a blood clot, having a stroke or a heart attack by as much as 50 percent! This is why more men have heart attacks in the mornings before 11 a.m. than at any other time of the day. This is a good reason to exercise between the hours of 6 p.m. to 8 p.m. if you are just starting an exercise routine. Your body is at its peak performance level at this time of day, muscles are loose, blood flow is optimal.

Slowly warming up your blood and stretching your veins and gradually increasing your blood circulation will allow your body to adjust to the strains you're about to put it through. I always jump rope slowly for three minutes, then stretch for 10 minutes and then I do some light cardio for three to five minutes to increase my heart rate. This makes me ready to begin any exercise routine.

You should also remember to do 10 minutes of cool down stretching after exercising. This is when you should do your deep stretches. Your muscles are warm and full of blood, which prevents improper tearing. The after stretching keeps your muscles flexible and helps keep you injury free.

Brace yourself

When I began working out, I quickly realized that I needed some extra support. Not just personal support, but in the form of braces. I purchased two knee braces, a wrist brace, an ankle brace, and a weight belt. When you're overweight, everything winds up hurting no matter what you do. I found that, by using these support devices, I could comfortably do most exercises. As I became stronger and lost some weight, I didn't need these braces as much. Now I only need the weight belt on heavy-lifting days. If you know you've got a weak knee, get a brace BEFORE you start exercising. If you've got a weak back, there are several types of braces available. Get the types of braces you need and wear them.

After the fact

You've done it. You've finished the big workout and know you're going to be sore tomorrow. What can you do to limit the pain and soreness? The trick is ice, heat, water, massage, supplements, and maybe a few pain inhibitors.

Ice therapy

You've seen it used during boxing matches and on football and baseball players after the game. These athletes get iced down with big bags of ice. It's all about controlling swelling and inflammation. Cold compresses decrease blood flow and numb the sensation of pain. The quicker you apply ice after working out, the better results you'll experience. You should apply ice to any joint or area you feel is strained or hurting. Only keep the ice on the hurting area for 10 to 15 minutes at a time.

Using varying sizes - small, medium, and large ice pack is important as it allows you to hit target areas. You should get at least two of each for two knees, two elbows, etc. Be sure to buy ice packs before you need them and get different types of ice holders. There are reuseable ice packs with velcro straps that work great. I also use several Ace® bandages to ensure that the packs stay in place.

I also suggest that you get instant cold packs for emergencies. Keep them in your gym bag, your car, home, and even at the office.

Heat therapy

After you've applied ice, try following up with a heat treatment. Heat increases overall circulation. The increased blood flow helps remove the accumulation of lactic acid, which is the main cause of pain, and reduces stiffness and muscle aches.

There are a large assortment of hot water bottles, instant heat packs, microwavable and electric heating pads available. I again suggest that you buy two of each. There are dry and moist heat. Try both to see which you prefer. Heating ointments and balms can be helpful too, even if they're a bit smelly.

Medical patches and pain inhibitors

My doctor introduced me to a wonderful thing called a Flector® patch. This is a small cloth adhesive patch that is treated with a pain inhibiter that gets absorbed through the skin. This patch works right where you need it. It's truly amazing. Once I started boxing and running 20 miles a week, this patch proved to be a real lifesaver for me. A doctor must prescribe it for you, so make sure you are really going to be sticking with a workout routine before you ask for it.

Saunas, steam rooms, and massage

Rewards! I count all of these as rewards. After every workout, I hit the sauna for at least 15 minutes. The dry heat is so good for you. It helps me unwind, and I treat it as my reward for a good workout. Steam rooms can be just as relaxing and beneficial as they open up your pores and help remove toxins.

I get one-to two-hour massages at least two times a month. If you've never experienced a real deep-tissue massage, I highly recommend it. This by far, is the most rewarding and beneficial repair work I do for my body and mind. Try several massage therapists to find one who works with your body type and who wants to help you reach your weight goals. Massage therapy is also a wonderful recovery tool when injured.

P.S. If you go get a massage with a female therapist, do not refer to her as a "masseuse." The term is now frowned upon by professional therapists who feel it refers to more seedy type of massage parlors. Always be a gentleman and tip your therapist.

Hot tubs and pools

Ahh, the hot tub, an exerciser's best friend. I can't tell you the hours I've spent soaking in the hot tub. It has made all of the exercising worthwhile. If you don't have access to one, find a gym or spa that offers one with your membership.

I promise you, it's worth every penny you spend to have access to it. It does wonders on sore muscles, helps put you to sleep at night, and warms you up on stiff achy mornings. If you have access to a pool, it can be great therapy also. Swimming is a fantastic stretching exercise. A good swim is invigorating and great for elongating and creating a lean look to your body. It's also the lowest impact exercise you can do. The cool water also reduces inflammation throughout the body.

Chain Breaker: Remember, it's essential that you learn and use several pain-avoidance techniques and proper pain management to ensure your success. Warm up and stretch properly before, and cool down after, each workout. Use braces where and when needed. Invest in and use several different sizes of ice and heat packs, then use them frequently. Use pain inhibitors when needed. Reward yourself with saunas, steam rooms, and massages. Soak in a hot tub every chance you get and try to swim a few laps as often as you can. These are the best pain avoidance tricks I've found.

I want you really pissed off about the decisions you've made.

I just hung up the phone. It was my dad on the other end of the line. Maybe at the end of his line, too. He called from the hospital. He was taken there with massive internal bleeding from his colon. This wasn't the first time he's been hospitalized in the past year, either. It's become like a second home for him, five times this year alone. The list of ailments he's suffering with is staggering. The amount of medications he is taking is just as ludicrous. All of it is because of bad decisions.

Not decisions he's making now. He doesn't get to make them any more. He gave up that freedom years and years ago. Doctors make the life extending decisions for him now. At 79 years old, it saddens and angers me that the ignorance, hunger, and poor decision-making of his past has shaped and determined his future.

Please understand that I originally wanted to make the last chapter of this book an uplifting, positive, strongly motivational one encouraging and inspiring you to take action and change your life for the better starting this very day. Then I thought about the actual nature of men our age. It takes a lot to move us into action. The fact is that if you read something motivational, you might be inspired for a few days. More than likely though, you would forget these fine words after a couple of weeks.

I've come to realize that what really moves men our age is anger. If we feel like we've been wronged, abused, or mistreated in some way, we get angry. It's only then that we actually get motivated to do something about it.

I know this to be the truth. I've tried many a diet only to quit. I've tried to become more active only to fall back into my old habits. What made it different this time? What's been the secret to making it work for me now? Anger. It was anger that made me want to change my life. Understand I'm not an angry man by nature, far, far from it. But when I was in that hospital bed five years ago, it was my laziness and bad decisions that had put me there. It was 100% my choices that led me to that place. Lying there in the ER, I got angry. Really furious. I was angry that I'd let myself go. Angry that I had believed it was all just part of getting older. Angry at my ridiculous decisions, blatant ignorance about the foods I was putting in my body, and lack of understanding about how important staying in good health is. I see now that it was my anger that actually moved me. I also understand that I never got over this anger. It's been my anger that pulled me through, time after time. It is not a bad anger or a hurtful anger, it's a righteous anger.

That day in the hospital, I thought of my old uncle, the Baptist preacher. I recalled a sermon he once gave about how Jesus entered the Temple only to find sellers and money changers polluting God's Temple, turning it into a den of thieves. I realized that I'd let sellers and money changers -- the giant restaurant chains, greedy corporations and corrupt pharmaceutical companies -- turn my body, which the Bible says is God's Temple, into a den of thieves, too. Thieves that only wanted to rob me of everything I held dear.

In the sermon, Jesus got angry, and was filled with anger. The Temple was his Father's house, a sacred and holy place. He couldn't stand for the thieves to be there, stealing everything he held dear for one more second. He made the decision to take action! He grabbed a staff and thrashed the place, busting it up, cleaning house, and running the thieves out for good. Did he make the priest mad? I'm sure he did. Did he offend some people? You bet. But it had to be done to restore health and purity to his Father's Temple. He had righteous anger. It's not a bad thing to have, although it's often misunderstood.

I am full of righteous anger even today. By righteous anger I mean perfectly wonderful, fine, and genuinely the morally justifiable feeling that I've been tricked, fooled, and deceived. That huge corporations, society, and mostly my own ignorant decisions made me massively overweight, sick, and suffering to the point that I almost lost everything I believed important to me: my wife, my daughter, my family, and my friends that I hold so dear. I am enraged that I almost lost MY LIFE just by eating.

The title of this book is *Fat as My Dad*. I named it this because at 45 years old, I'd become as unhealthy, sick, and fat as my dad was at 75. I knew that because, of my poor decisions up until that point, the odds were I'd never get the chance to see my 75th birthday.

The simple fact that you've just read this book tells me that you too are as fat as your dad, or maybe even fatter. I'm sure you've watched your self-esteem vanish right before your eyes. Maybe you have become an invisible man to your family, friends, and what seems like the whole world. Today is the day for change in your life.

I want to make you angry. I want you to build a powerful, righteous anger deep within you, one that burns at your insides every day! An anger that makes you say...
"I'm not going to die from being overweight. It will not happen to me!"

Decide to stop making bad choices about your life and your health. Determine at this moment that you won't be invisible, broken, sick, sad, and disheartened another day. Tell yourself, "I will no longer accept this unhealthy fate forced upon me by a warped, uncaring, unconcerned, profit hungry society. I will not go quietly. I'm going to fight. I will make a difference in this world!"

Below are the words I wrote myself when I started my weight-loss journey. It's really a prayer, my mantra, a personal affirmation that I've read to myself many times to rebuild my resolve throughout my journey. As you read it, I want you to ask yourself this question... "Is this what I want from my life too?"

I want to live my life with everything I have in me. I want more from my life and I want it starting today. I want to learn and grow mentally, physically, and spiritually. I want to help others. I want to be a giver and not just a consumer. I want to find meaning in every breath I'm allowed to take. I want and need to love, forgive, and live more. I declare here and now that no pain or heartache, or past hurt or unjustness, will deter me.

I will be strong and healthy and wise for the rest of my life. And nothing... absolutely nothing except the will of God will make me stop, give up, surrender, fail, or fall short of what I know and believe I am completely capable of becoming. I am the possibility. Because what I believe about myself, it all comes true, and I'm going to believe the best about myself for the rest of my life.

Tim 2 Taylor

This is what I resolved to myself lying in that hospital bed, an already half-dead and dying man. From that moment on, I knew that if I was given a second chance at life, I was going to live it to the best of my ability. I pray that you realize and want these things for your life too. I pray that you realize and deserve a healthy body, a growing mind, and a powerful heart to shape your life for the better for the rest of your life. 2B4L – To be for life!

Chain Breaker: Look down at your belly don't fool yourself any longer. Look up and read this out loud:

"I'm angry. I am going to make the decision to take action right now. I'm going to pick just four Chain Breaker things I've learned by reading this book and make them a part of my new lifestyle starting now. I will re-read this book 28 days from now, and then add at least seven more things I've learned and put them into action. I will continue adding more tips every 28 days. I believe in myself and my abilities to do this."

Set small goals and reach them. Set at least one mountain top goal; i.e. lose 25, 50, or 100 pounds, or to run a marathon, whatever, just make it and write it down. Then decide to **never give up** and **never to go back** until you reach it. See yourself on a new road to a healthier destination starting today. See yourself becoming you again.

I want you to write to me, e-mail me, tweet me, send me pictures, inspire me with all the good you can do in this world. I **REALLY** want to see what you can do. Start writing the number "2" on everything to remind yourself you are on your second life now. And believe me, the best is yet 2 come in your life. God Bless You.

What you believe about yourself... it all comes true. Believe the best!

Tim 2 Taylor

Dietary Supplements
Vitamins and Minerals I Take

WARNING: YOU SHOULD NEVER START ANY SUPPLEMENTS WITHOUT CONSULTING WITH A PHYSICIAN FIRST. Supplements should not be an absolute thing for anyone. Your body is constantly changing and you should address it's needs on an individual basis, especially if you are taking other prescription drugs.

Amino Acids - 24 grams - just before and during workouts
Acidophilus Pearls (probiotic) - 1 pill a day - at night just before bed
Biotin - 5000 mcg -1 pills a day - at lunch
Calcium - Mineral - 1000 mg or 1 cup of milk at night just before bed
CLA - 1000mg - 2 pills a day - at night just before bed
Coleus Forskohlii -125 mg - 1 pill a day at night just before bed
CoQ10 -100mg - 1 pill a day in the morning
Dehydroepiandrosterone (DHEA) -10 mg -1 pill a day at lunch
Flax Seed Oil -1000 mg -1 pill a day - at night just before bed
GABA - 750 mg - 2 pills a day - at night just before bed
Green Tea - 400mg - 1 pill a day in the morning - (most of the time I just drink a cup of tea)
Gamma-Linolenic Acid (GLA) - 500 mg -1 pill a day in the morning
HMB - 200 mg - 4 pills - right after a workout
Iron - Mineral -15 mg -1 pill a day at lunch
L-Carnitine - 1 pill a day in the morning
Lopoic Acid - 266 mg -1 pill a day in the morning
Magnesium - 400 mg - 1 pill in the morning and 2 at night
Niacin (Vitamin B-3) -100 mg - half a pill in the morning - half in the afternoon
Omega 3 Fatty Acids EPA-DHA (A MUST) - 1000 mg -2 pills at night before bed
Policosanol - 20 mg -1 pill a day in the morning
Potassium - Mineral 250 mg - 1 pill every other day at lunch
Phosphatidylserine - 1000 mg - 1 pill just before workouts
R-ALA -Alpha Lipoic Acid - 200 mg -2 pills before a work out
Saw Palmetto 320 mg -1 pill a day in the morning
Tribulus Terrestris with Avena Sativa - 1 pill a day at night just before bed
Vitamin A (Dry A) - 5000 IU -1 pill a day in the morning
Vitamin B-6 - 100 mg - 2 pills a day in the morning
Vitamin B-12 - 1 shot a week
Vitamin C - 240 mg - 2 pills a day in the morning
Vitamin D - 200 IU - 2 pills a day at night just before bed
Vitamin E - 400 IU - 1 pill a day in the morning
Vitamin K2 - 100 IU - 1 pill a day in the morning
Zinc - Mineral -15 mg - 1 pill a day at lunch
Mega Men SPORT multivitamin - 2 pills a day in the morning

Human Emotions

Here is the list of both positive (56) and negative (63) human emotions. You can copy this page and use it as a check-list to chart your emotions just before you eat anything. Remember to track every time you eat anything. Keep track for 28 days without looking back at past days. Wait untill you have completed 28 days to tabulate your results. This will give you more accurate results and a clearer picture to gauge your emotions as they pertain to eating habits.

Date: /   /   B = Breakfast   L = Lunch   D = Dinner

POSITIVE EMOTIONS

B L D
☐☐☐ Able
☐☐☐ Adequate
☐☐☐ Assured
☐☐☐ Awe
☐☐☐ Capable
☐☐☐ Certain
☐☐☐ Cheerful
☐☐☐ Charmed
☐☐☐ Comfortable
☐☐☐ Compassion
☐☐☐ Confidence
☐☐☐ Courageous
☐☐☐ Delighted
☐☐☐ Determined
☐☐☐ Eager
☐☐☐ Elation
☐☐☐ Empathy
☐☐☐ Energetic
☐☐☐ Enthusiastic
☐☐☐ Excellent
☐☐☐ Excited
☐☐☐ Exhilarated
☐☐☐ Expectant
☐☐☐ Fascinated
☐☐☐ Glad
☐☐☐ Glamorous
☐☐☐ Glorious
☐☐☐ Graceful

B L D
☐☐☐ Grateful
☐☐☐ Great
☐☐☐ Good
☐☐☐ Happy
☐☐☐ Hopeful
☐☐☐ Humorous
☐☐☐ Inspired
☐☐☐ Interested
☐☐☐ Joyful
☐☐☐ Magnificent
☐☐☐ Lust
☐☐☐ Love
☐☐☐ Peaceful
☐☐☐ Pleasant
☐☐☐ Pleasure
☐☐☐ Playfulness
☐☐☐ Positive
☐☐☐ Powerful
☐☐☐ Pride
☐☐☐ Relaxed
☐☐☐ Relieved
☐☐☐ Satisfied
☐☐☐ Stable
☐☐☐ Sublime
☐☐☐ Superior
☐☐☐ Surprised
☐☐☐ Sympathy
☐☐☐ Thrilled

NEGATIVE EMOTIONS

B L D
☐☐☐ Agonize
☐☐☐ Anger
☐☐☐ Annoyed
☐☐☐ Anxiety
☐☐☐ Anxious
☐☐☐ Apathy
☐☐☐ Apprehensive
☐☐☐ Bored
☐☐☐ Burdened
☐☐☐ Cautious
☐☐☐ Competitive
☐☐☐ Concerned
☐☐☐ Confused
☐☐☐ Contempt
☐☐☐ Depressed
☐☐☐ Destructive
☐☐☐ Disappointed
☐☐☐ Disgusted
☐☐☐ Distracted
☐☐☐ Doubtful
☐☐☐ Embarrassment
☐☐☐ Envy
☐☐☐ Exasperated
☐☐☐ Exhausted
☐☐☐ Fear
☐☐☐ Frustrated
☐☐☐ Greed
☐☐☐ Grief
☐☐☐ Guilty
☐☐☐ Harassed
☐☐☐ Hesitant
☐☐☐ Hostile

B L D
☐☐☐ Ignored
☐☐☐ Impatient
☐☐☐ Indifferent
☐☐☐ Intimidated
☐☐☐ Isolated
☐☐☐ Irritated
☐☐☐ Jealous
☐☐☐ Jumpy
☐☐☐ Lonely
☐☐☐ Mad
☐☐☐ Manipulated
☐☐☐ Miserable
☐☐☐ Obnoxious
☐☐☐ Overwhelmed
☐☐☐ Panic
☐☐☐ Pressured
☐☐☐ Remorse
☐☐☐ Revenge
☐☐☐ Shame
☐☐☐ Sad
☐☐☐ Scared
☐☐☐ Shocked
☐☐☐ Stress
☐☐☐ Suspicious
☐☐☐ Tired
☐☐☐ Uncomfortable
☐☐☐ Uneasy
☐☐☐ Used
☐☐☐ Wary
☐☐☐ Weary
☐☐☐ Wasteful

Products I use.

I haven't been paid to endorse or recommend any of these products. It's just that I've used these products over the last 5 years, and they have proven to be effective with my health and weight-loss . They might be helpful for you too.

V8 Fusion Light

The Vitamin Shoppe
Fish Oil

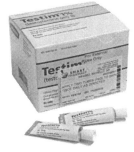

Testim® Testosterone
Replacement

www.v8juice.com

www.vitaminshoppe.com

www.testim.com

Acidophilus Pearls
Probiotic Supplement

Amino Vital

P90X Extreme Workout
For use only after weight loss
and in top phyical condition.

www.pearlslife.com

www.amino-vital.com

www.beachbody.com

Protein types I use daily.

All my mixed shakes have one full scoop of Whey Protein Isolate and half a scoop of Casein for a total of 39 grams per shake (2 times a day = 78 grams). My after-workout protein drink is 30 grams, then my Casein shake is 24 grams, for a total of 132 grams per day from protein supplements.

At 1.5 grams per pound of body weight (205), I should be getting 307.5 grams a day. Proteins derived from eaten foods average 113 grams.

An example of a day's food intake:

7 oz chicken - 49 grams

1 cup milk - 8 grams

Oatmeal - 3 grams

7 oz Turkey - 49 grams

8 oz - OJ - 4 grams

Current daily intake is averaging 245 grams, leaving me 62 grams shy of a goal of 1.5 grams per pound.

Syntrax Nectar - Whey Protein Isolate (my favorite - features and flavors)

(27grams per scoop)

90 calories

0 calories fat

5mg cholesterol

60 mg sodium

120 mg Potassium

0 carbs

0 sugars

No Aspartame

www.si03.com

MuscleTech -Whey Protein Isolate

(28.5 grams per scoop)
110 calories
10 fat
45 mg cholesterol
70 mg sodium
140 mg Potassium
4.5 g carbs
2 grams sugars
Has Aspartame

www.muscletech.com

ON - Gold Standard Casein Protein

(24 grams per scoop)
120 calories
10 fat
10 mg cholesterol
220 mg sodium
3 g carbs
0 grams sugars
Has Aspartame

www.optimumnutrition.com

Designer Whey Protein Isolate (Premixed bottled - features and flavors)

I usually drink right after my workout.
(30 grams per bottle)
120 calories
0 calories fat
3 mg cholesterol
45 mg sodium
140 mg Potassium
1 carb
1 sugar
No Aspartame
- does have Sucralose

www.designerwhey.com

Lifetime Tips

• You've heard the saying " Life is not a destination... it's a journey." That has proven to be so true. Every day I've found that you have to think about the journey to being fit, healthy, stronger and staying in control of your mind, body and spirit ... basically your life.

• Every day it's about choices (constantly making better ones). It's what I call "Little Victories." Every time I choose a healthier food, choose to do my exercise, choose to be positive it's a little victory, and little victories can win the war. Believe me, it's the little things that really matter.

• Stay healthy to stay on target. Don't run a marathon in your first, second, or sixth month. Give yourself time to get used to your new lifestyle. Basically, stay smart, don't over-do it. Give your body time to heal. If injured, get professional help to heal, and heal slowly. Don't let it stop you. Negativity and injuries will be two of the most dangerous things stopping you from achieving your goals.

• Reinvent everything about yourself. Continually re-adjust your goals, and re-adjust your dreams. You'll find you'll be less disappointed and more optimistic. Let go of your old habits and embrace the new. It will keep you young and full of life.

• Weight loss is not just about food! (Yeah it's one part, but there is so much more.) I have found that it's three main parts -

>   1. Head, Heart (*emotions and commitment*), and Spirit.
>   2. Stomach, Food, and Portions.
>   3. Movement, Motivation, Management.

• Look for, ask for, and use all the help you can find, from friends, spouses, co-workers, personal trainers, classes, and groups, TV shows, websites, apps, books, blogs, DVDs, magazines – whatever. Use it all!

• Realize failures, set-backs, and mistakes are a **very real** part of being human. Learn from them. Never let them paralyze or derail your dreams or keep you from reaching your goals. We all fail, we all fall, we all get knocked down. Getting back up shows your heart!

• Three days off your plan can spoil your week. A week off can make you fall back into old ways. My advice, always catch yourself on day three. Then re-double your efforts, re-focus on what you want to have happen in your life, and make it so.

• The human body is a truly amazing thing. It wants constantly to stay balanced, poorly or rightly, but it will always try to bring you back to a balance. Forcing it to readjust (every 28 days) has made it easier to stay at goal weight. If you give it the right balance of respect, nutrition, and exercise, it will come back to a proper balance for you every time. Neglect any one of these and you'll have a hard time – every time.

• Learn! Then learn to let go of the past. I've found that anchors stuck in the mucky depths of the past keep so many people from setting a new course, raising a new sail in the wind, and steering toward a new destination – much less starting a journey. If you need some help letting go, it's OK to seek professional help (a psychiatrist, psychologist, or a therapist) so by all means get it. I did, and it played a vital role in my long term success emotionally and mentally.

• Smile at others more. Laugh with others more. Give to others more and just see what you'll get in return. I'm telling you it's the best thing in life!

• Pay more (good, prime) attention to yourself (mentally, spiritually, physically). It can be as simple as grooming, brushing your teeth, getting a new pair of shoes, a stylish shirt, meditation or prayer. It's ESSENTIAL and good to be good to yourself.

• When you reach a goal, and you're on the mountaintop get out your binoculars and look as far out as you can to set your next goal. Remember... it's not a destination... it's a journey! Make it as fun and as lively as you can.

• Try new foods. There is a HUGE world of tastes out there. Become BOLD, because you'll never know unless you go! I've had a thousand new "YUCK" moments in the past four years. I didn't die... but I did find a lot of new, healthier foods I now love.

• Refuse to be invisible! Realize you are important, vital and vibrant. Never allow some-one to hurt you, verbally, mentally or physically. You **are not** your weight. You deserve the best life has to offer. Go and get it.

• Daily make it OCCUR to you. I spell it "AKIR" - Always Keep It Real! If you are fooling yourself about your own life, STOP IT TODAY. This is your ONLY life, here... right now. It's everything! It can be that magic moment right now... Carpe diem!

• If you like to eat - Then make MUSCLES you new goal. Every pound of muscle you build on your body burns 35 to 50 calories a day. Anyone... ANYONE can add muscle. No excuses! The benefits are astounding.

• You have 168 hours in every week. All you need to become healthier is 3 of those hours a week. That's only 180 minutes. The average American is awake 17 hours a day – that's 119 waking hours a week. All you need is 22.9 minutes of each day to make things happen. Find some way to capture that time. Aren't you worth it? Your health and happiness? You CAN find 22.9 minutes (11.9 minutes in the morning and 11 minutes at night.) to get some exercise – just do it!

• ALWAYS know what you are going to eat for every meal and snack a day in advance. NEVER wait until 15 or 30 minutes before ANY meal to decide what or where to eat. You know you're going to eat tomorrow – decide in advance today. You will always make better, healthier choices. Doing this completely kills impulse eating.

• Listen to good, positive music when you workout and during your day. It will make your workout easier and put positive vibes into your life.

Tim 2's Weight Loss Stats

• On 8/6/05 I weighed 272 pounds at my heart doctor's office.

• On 9/8/05 - I joined Weight Watchers, weighing in at 261.2 pounds

• The night I hit my Goal Weight, 8/24/06, I weighed in at – 199 pounds

• 62.2 pounds lost (actually 73 pounds total lost) As of August 2006 I'd lost a total of 89 lbs and I weighed in at 183)

• So in 50 weeks that's an average of 1.24 pounds a week!
  (2 weeks short of a year)

• 6 of those weeks I actually GAINED Weight!

• 5 of those weeks I lost less than half of a pound.

• So 50 weeks minus the 11 weeks of gains or very minor losses equals
  39 weeks of actual losses, which averages out to just 1.7 pounds a week.
  So you see It doesn't take very much to make a HUGE difference!

Acknowledgments

I've spent the last 5 years researching, testing, writing, and re-writing this book several times. It's been a labor, I wish I could say of pure love – in some ways it was if you consider the labor involved was actually like birthing a baby. I specifically wrote this book for men of a certain age to quickly grasp the tried and tested things I learned through these years of many trials and errors, blood, sweat, and tears... to finally achieve success and keep it in my life.

Many people have assisted me in arriving at the completion of this book. I want to give unyielding gratitude to my wife and daughter for their support and for putting up with me throughout my whole weight loss/fitness journey.

My true friends, you know exactly who you are and why you are my indeed my friend. Surely you know why I am yours - throughout time and tide.

My personal physician, Dr. Michelle Mendez D.O. whose medical assistance has been invaluable to me along this treacherous trip. My therapists, who have helped me find emotional stability and mental clarity during the tough and trying times.

To all my personal trainers, from the first one - Benny, who pulled me out of a dark workout room at the gym and helped me see it was okay to exercise with others fighting the same battle as me. My boxing trainers, James Smiley and Matt Vona, who tought me how to find courage and heart to stay in the fight.

My bodybuilding trainers, Don and Sarah Long, who helped me to push harder no matter the odds. My massage therapist, Jennifer, and my physical therapist Liz who helped me in my many healings and recoveries over these many sore, sprained, torn, broken and often painful yet exhilarating years.

Karen, my Weight Watchers leader, who helped me believe in myself one small step, one pound at a time. The great legal team at Smith, Gambrel, and Russell, specifically Kate Rowe and Kathy Hennessey for all there endless extensions on my behalf.

Renowned motivational speaker, Curtis Zimmerman, for helping me to get in the pool and become an "Olympic" swimmer. And all my super friends from NSA!

Finally I wish to thank the simple kindness of the people I've encountered on my journey who went out of their way to help me become a better person and inspired me to give back to others. Their simple kindness has truly made all the difference.

And lastly my Lord and Savior Jesus Christ.

Postscript WOLF note

On September 5, 2010, I experienced a severe motorcycle accident. I flew over the handlebars and my elbow went into my ribs breaking seven of them. Two of the ribs broke completely off in two different places. Needless to say, I was in very bad shape. No surgeons would touch me, no specialist could help me. I went through so many doctors, CAT scans, MRI's, X-rays and procedures I've lost track.

But three weeks later I was up and around again. All of my doctors couldn't believe it. They had seen patients with less severe injuries be sidelined for a year or more. Yet there I was picking up my life. And what did my doctors accredit it to? The physical and mental condition I was in at the time of the accident - 100 %. But I know it was the simple grace of God saving me yet again.

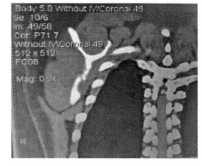

In the ten months since the accident, most of my ribs have healed. The bad news is two have not, and only time will tell with them. I haven't been able to really workout at all. This has taken a toll on me for sure. But on the morning of the accident weighed in at 205 pounds. Today I weigh 213. Am I scared I'll gain all my weight back after keeping it off for over 5 years? No, I'm not at all.

I've learned that life is full of setbacks and difficulties. I've encountered many a road block and failures by the thousands in my life. I've dealt with hundreds of blows to my body while I was boxing, so I know how to deal with pain. It's called finding and keeping heart.

Listen, If you mistakenly think that once you're on the mountaintop you will always stay there – here's is a news flash – you won't. There are always going to be new valleys. It's in these deep valleys that you'll find the truest of friends, the dearest of loved ones, and life's best lessons will be learned. In these valleys, you learn who you are and what you are really made of, to actually know if what you really believe is truth.

I wanted to share this with you because getting older is fraught with changes, unexpected twists and seriously hard turns. But it's nothing you and I can't handle. I believe in me, so you believe in you and we'll make it over!

I want you to find courage, be strong, seek help and never give up hope. Do anything you can to keep your dreams and your heart alive. Keep climbing, and that uphill tread will always lead you back to another mountaintop. Remember the world is a random and dangerous place. Stay sharp and hopefully you won't ever get bitten.

Tomorrow I'm going back to the gym for the first time in over nine months. Will it be a mountaintop experience? Maybe, but then again maybe not. But it's one step up. One step forward to becoming the man I know I can be. And I'm sending this book off to the publishers today. For me that's good enough for the day. – God Bless, Tim 2 Taylor